POCKET STUDY SKILLS

Kate Williams and Mary Davis

REFERENCING & UNDERSTANDING PLAGIARISM

SECOND EDITION

T0191126

macmillan
international
HIGHER EDUCATION

RED GLOBE
PRESS

First edition 2009
Second edition 2017

First published 2009 by
PALGRAVE

Red Globe Press in the UK is an imprint of Macmillan Publishers Limited,
registered in England, company number 785998, of 4 Crinan Street,
London, N1 9XW.

Red Globe Press® is a registered trademark in the United States, the
United Kingdom, Europe and other countries.

ISBN 978–1–137–53071–4 paperback

This book is printed on paper suitable for recycling and made from fully
managed and sustained forest sources. Logging, pulping and manufacturing
processes are expected to conform to the environmental regulations of the
country of origin.

A catalogue record for this book is available from the British Library.

A catalog record for this book is available from the Library of Congress.

Contents

Acknowledgements

Many people have contributed to this guide – both to the original book and to this revised and updated edition – and we would like to thank them all. First, thanks to students who have discussed queries and dilemmas with us and special thanks to the students whose work appears here: Alex, Nuri, Peter and Phivos.

We are most grateful to critical readers of the first edition, who have pointed out their favourite pages and made suggestions for this new edition.

We are grateful to Jude Carroll for her valuable contribution to the first edition. Thanks also to colleagues at Oxford Brookes University: to Richard Persaud (Library) for his advice and sharp eye for detail, and colleagues at the Upgrade study advice service, for sharing their insights into referencing dilemmas.

The authors and publisher wish to thank the following for their kind permission to reproduce their materials: Carly Dove and Gill Rowell at Turnitin, Dr John Morley at the University of Manchester for the use of Academic Phrasebank and Dolores Campanario at WHO.

Thanks too to Sallie Godwin for her astute illustrations and to Suzannah Burywood, Helen Caunce and colleagues in the editing and production teams at Palgrave for their supportive and creative work with us.

Introduction

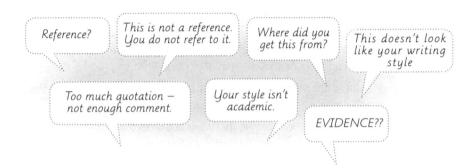

If you have ever had feedback like this on your work and wondered what it means and what you should do about it, then this guide is for you.

Comments like these suggest two things:
- you need to get to grips with referencing
- you are not yet confident about how to draw on other writers and sources in your own writing.

This book is designed to show you:

- how to reference, both in your work and in your reference list
- how to write with confidence: to be able to discuss the work of other writers, and use it to shape the points you want to make in your work
- what plagiarism is and how it can happen. It shows you how to develop good study habits and skills so you don't have to worry about plagiarising by accident.

This new edition has been extensively revised and updated with new extracts and examples reflecting changes both in referencing norms and practices and in understanding plagiarism. Technology has introduced a whole new raft of opportunities to develop good study habits with new online resources and reference management tools. It has also created many more choices and dilemmas with the help you can get and more opportunities for poor practice in study. **Your work must always be your work!**

About this book

The Harvard referencing style is used throughout Parts 1–4 of the book. Part 5 illustrates the use of four other styles used in particular subject areas.

Part 1: Understanding referencing gives an overview of what referencing is, why it matters and how it is part of the overall task of understanding, researching (and using referencing tools), planning and writing an assignment.

Part 2: Writing and referencing shows you how to use sources in your writing, the language to use when you refer to a source – summarising, paraphrasing and more.

Part 3: Understanding plagiarism shows you the steps to take in doing 'your own work', good practice in getting help, and how some tools can change your work so it's not really yours. Test your understanding with the quizzes and learn about Turnitin (Feedback Studio).

Part 4: Referencing: the practicalities starts with answers to frequent questions, and gives examples of how to reference the most frequently used sources, both in your text and how to list it in your reference list.

Part 5: Other referencing styles outlines the use of four other styles used in particular subject areas: Vancouver, MHRA, APA and MLA.

UNDERSTANDING REFERENCING

Part 1 gives an overview of what referencing is, why it matters and how it is part of the overall task of understanding, researching (and using referencing tools), planning and writing an assignment.

What's different about writing at university?

Quite a lot is different. That's true no matter where you studied before.

Universities are research environments. Most tutors and lecturers do research of some sort and base their writing on the style used in the books, articles and reports they read for their research: that's where they, too, publish. So it follows that students are also expected to develop the 'academic' style that matches their field of study.

So what is UK 'academic' style?

Well, of course, it varies from subject to subject – dance, science and business are massively different, so the style of writing expected in different areas of study will vary too. But let's try a few generalisations!

You are NOT expected to:
▶ Write out facts, describe events, and just summarise your reading or lectures (unless you are expressly asked to – for example, to draw up a timeline, outline, describe a process or observation or do a 'summary').

You ARE expected to:
▶ Consider a question or topic from several angles: if you are asked to 'outline' different theories, studies or interpretations of 'facts' or events, you will almost certainly be expected to 'discuss' or 'evaluate' them too.

You are ALWAYS expected to:
▶ Show the EVIDENCE for the statements you make. You will need evidence if the statement is a 'fact', or mentions the approach of a particular writer, or describes the findings of a study.

So on to referencing

You provide evidence by telling the reader about the source of your information. The reference is the link between what you write and the evidence on which your writing is based. It turns what you write from being just your thoughts and reactions into something that links your ideas with the writings of other people who have thought and written about the same issue. It is how you carry out and share your research process.

This chapter gives a quick overview of why and how to reference. From here you can read on through Part 1 to get a better understanding of referencing as central to your research and writing. Or you can decide to fast forward to another part of the book. You can always come back later!

Reference, reference, reference – why do I have to reference everything?

The one overarching reason why you need to reference is to show your reader where the evidence for what you say has come from. This will enable them to:

▶ go and check the source themselves – **traceability**
▶ understand the nature, strengths and limitations of your source – **authority** and **credibility**
▶ form their own view about the source and the use you make of it – **reliability**.

The reader will also be able to see:

▶ the range of sources you have found and used, from textbooks to the reading list and beyond – **reach** and **scope**

▶ your acknowledgment of the value of the efforts and findings of others –
politeness.

All this feeds into your reader's impression of your competence as a researcher and
your 'professionalism' as a student. Your tutor will approach your work feeling positive –
and that has got to be a good thing!

What does your reader need to know? The bare essentials

The six **strategic questions**[1] make a useful checklist of the information you need to
know about your source.

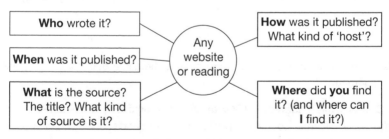

---

1 See *Getting critical*, 2nd edn, in this series, p2 and pp30–7 for how to use the strategic questions
to evaluate sources.

The answers you need to give to your reader in your reference are:

Rachel Aldred and Katrina Jungnickel wrote an article (published) in **2014**. The title is **Why culture matters for transport policy: the case of cycling in the UK**. It was published in the *Journal of Transport Geography* in **volume 34**, the **January** edition, on **pages 78–87**. And this is where you can find it: doi:10.1016/j.jtrangeo.2013.11.004.

In reference form (author-year Harvard style), this becomes:

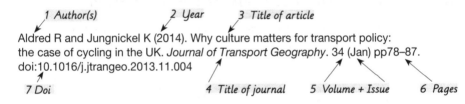

1 Author(s)   *2 Year*   *3 Title of article*

Aldred R and Jungnickel K (2014). Why culture matters for transport policy:
the case of cycling in the UK. *Journal of Transport Geography*. 34 (Jan) pp78–87.
doi:10.1016/j.jtrangeo.2013.11.004

7 Doi   *4 Title of journal*   *5 Volume + Issue*   *6 Pages*

All referencing styles provide details that answer the same questions – they are just set out differently.

> **The Digital Object Identifier (DOI or doi)** is a unique and permanent number used to identify sources, especially academic and scholarly articles, research reports and datasets, and official or government publications. The DOI will take you directly to the source or 'object' in a search.

Help your reader to find your source

It isn't good enough just to list everything you have read for an assignment at the end of your writing. At best this just tells your reader that you've been busy; at worst it gives the impression that you've borrowed a list from somewhere else. Your reader will just get annoyed (*'where did she get this from?'*) and you will be the loser.

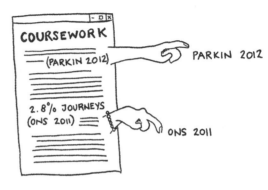

The whole purpose of referencing is to make the process of tracking back to previous research as clear as possible. **Point** your reader to where they can find the support for particular statements at the exact point you draw on the source.

How referencing works

There are many different referencing styles, and many more local variations. All operate on the same principles of two linked elements.

In your text you drop in a signal at the point in your writing where you use a source. This is a 'citation'. It tells the reader two things:

1 that the idea, point or evidence comes from your research
2 where to look for more information on that source.

The signal is either:

- a **number**[1] or [1] in numeric systems, or
- the **author + year** of publication in (most) author-date systems.

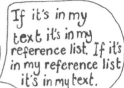

If it's in my text it's in my reference list. If it's in my reference list it's in my text.

In your reference list at the end of your work include ALL the sources you use, giving full details of where to find them. The list can be in either:

- **number order** according to where you first use that source in your text (numeric style), or
- **alphabetical order** by the author's last name (surname/family name) or name of the organisation (author-date style).

Whichever style you use, make sure:

- every source you cite in your work is listed in your references giving the details of where YOU found it
- every source listed in your references section is cited in your work.

Styles of referencing

Different disciplines have their preferred way of referencing, often with good reason, sometimes by convention. As a newcomer to the subject, clearly you should follow the models. Some styles have quite precise expectations about how a reference is set out (MLA for example). Others are more flexible about layout and punctuation. However, even within one subject area – sometimes even in the same department – there can be differences. Individual tutors tend to want students to set out references in the way they themselves do.

All this makes for conflicting advice and confusion for students. What's OK on one module can be marked as wrong on another. The upshot is that referencing is confusing for many people, and, worse still, students (and tutors!) often fail to distinguish between what is important in referencing and what is not.

They are all correct!

Harvard, the style most used in the UK, has no definitive handbook, so there are lots of variations in style – and they are all correct!

ALDRED, R. and JUNGNICKEL, K. (2014). Why culture matters for transport policy: the case of cycling in the UK. *Journal of Transport Geography*. No 34 (Jan) pp78–87.

Aldred, R. and Jungnickel, K. 2014. Why Culture Matters for Transport Policy: the Case of Cycling in the UK. *Journal of Transport Geography*. Vol. 34, January, pp78–87. doi:10.1016/j.jtrangeo.2013.11.004.

Aldred R and Jungnickel K (2014). 'Why culture matters for transport policy: the case of cycling in the UK'. *J Trans Geog 34* (Jan): 78–87. Available at … . (Accessed … date)

They have all been modelled on books and articles published by major publishers and they are all absolutely correct! The Pocket series style uses the least punctuation of all. This too is perfectly correct!

So what do you do?

Try a bit of self-preservation! Find out how your reader/tutor/editor wants you to set out your references – and set them out in exactly that way!

Your module/course handbook will almost certainly state how they want this done. Keep this handy when you are writing, and follow the models. Exactly.

What matters and what doesn't?

It doesn't matter if you:

- use or don't use commas, full stops, capitals in titles, underlining/italics. But **be consistent** because different patterns of punctuation annoy readers and could suggest you are overreliant on cut and paste
- can't track down some detail, despite your best efforts. It's better to refer to a good source and give the details you have than to leave it out because of a missing detail (see p121).

It does matter that you:

- understand the purpose of referencing
- place your in-text link ('citation') at the point you use a source
- give as full a set of details as you can about each source in your reference list
- give up the idea of 'hanging on' to the words used in your source, even if you feel they say it better than you do
- learn to integrate references into your writing style (see Chapter 2)
- pick one style of referencing and stick to it.

It is unrealistic, however, to expect students to be 100% accurate. World-class professors send books and articles to publishers with incomplete references and copy-editors check and correct missing reference details. Tutors will be looking for authenticity – wanting to see what you have really read and thought about this source material.

Referencing styles

This chapter outlines the main referencing styles used at university. Most courses will use a style from one of the two 'families' below, or local adaptations of these. You don't need to know them all – check the ones used in the courses you take.

Family 1: In-text name referencing styles

In your work cite the surname of the author(s) at the point you draw on a source.

In your reference list give the full details of each source in alphabetical order, so your reader can find it by surname of the first author.

This guide uses Harvard except where we explicitly state that we are giving examples of other styles (see Part 5).

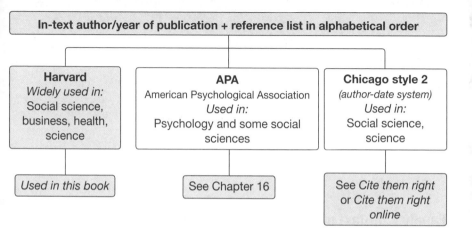

In-text author/year of publication + reference list in alphabetical order		
Harvard *Widely used in:* Social science, business, health, science	**APA** American Psychological Association *Used in:* Psychology and some social sciences	**Chicago style 2** *(author-date system)* *Used in:* Social science, science
Used in this book	See Chapter 16	See *Cite them right* or *Cite them right online*

A Harvard reference	
In your work	**In your reference list**
… similarly high levels [of cycling] were experienced in the Netherlands and Denmark (Pucher and Buehler 2008).	Pucher J and Buehler R (2008). Making cycling irresistible: lessons from the Netherlands, Denmark and Germany. *Transport Reviews*. 28 (4) pp495–528.

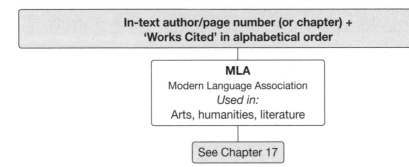

In-text author/page number (or chapter) +
'Works Cited' in alphabetical order

MLA
Modern Language Association
Used in:
Arts, humanities, literature

See Chapter 17

Family 2: In-text numerical styles

In your work you use a number, in superscript[3] or brackets, round (3) or square [3] at the point you draw on a source.

In your references give the full details of each source in numerical order, with the first source you use listed as 1, the second as 2 and so on.

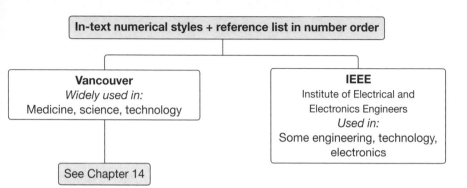

A Vancouver reference	
In your work	**In your reference list**
… similarly high levels [of cycling] were experienced in the Netherlands and Denmark.[7]	7 Pucher J and Buehler R. Making cycling irresistible: lessons from the Netherlands, Denmark and Germany. *Transp Rev*. 2008; 28 (4): 495–528.

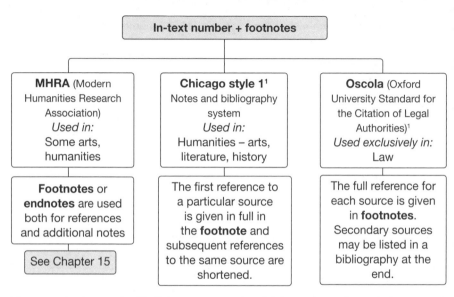

In-text number + footnotes

MHRA (Modern Humanities Research Association)
Used in:
Some arts, humanities

Chicago style 1[1]
Notes and bibliography system
Used in:
Humanities – arts, literature, history

Oscola (Oxford University Standard for the Citation of Legal Authorities)[1]
Used exclusively in:
Law

Footnotes or **endnotes** are used both for references and additional notes

See Chapter 15

The first reference to a particular source is given in full in the **footnote** and subsequent references to the same source are shortened.

The full reference for each source is given in **footnotes**. Secondary sources may be listed in a bibliography at the end.

You may also be required to list your sources in a bibliography at the end of your work.

1 For detailed guidance on this style, see *Cite them right*, 10th edn. See also *Cite them right online*, available via many university libraries.

Read your course materials carefully to make sure you are clear about the style of referencing your tutor expects for that particular module or course. You may well be given guidance and helpful models to use. If so, do use them!

Your reading list may include not only essential and additional chapters and articles, but links to useful databases and websites. Take a hint! If these sources are suggested, make sure you check them out and use some of them.

Your references will show your research footprints and be the record of your research. Record them carefully as you go, and connect each source with notes you make.

Referencing software can help with this: on to Chapter 3.

Referencing is a great invention. It enables researchers of all levels, from eminent professor to first-year student, to show and share their research with their readers. Your reader will be able to see how your research has informed your thinking and understanding.

Throughout your research, keep careful records, notes, and the full reference of every source you check out. You'll do a lot of work before you get anywhere near planning and writing your assignment or essay. Your references are the record of your research. Look after them!

Choosing your sources

Before you start looking for sources to research your assignment or essay, you need to be clear about what exactly the task or question is asking you. Different questions can be researched through different kinds of sources.

For tips on making effective notes, see *Reading and making notes*, 2nd edn, Parts 5 and 6, and for details on the stages of essay writing, see *Planning your essay*, 2nd edn, Ch. 2 (both in this series).

Books, journal articles and **websites** are the essential sources of information, ideas and interpretation. But you may need to consult other types of sources current in your subject area and relevant to your task.

For any source you have to decide if it is any good for your purpose.

company reports   online article   newspapers or magazines   Film

advertisements   **YouTube**   photos   **patents**

Conference proceedings   Statistics   **Leaflets**   Twitter

dissertations   Government policies   Legislation

Try using the <u>strategic questions</u> (see p5) as a checklist to help you evaluate the source and decide if you want to explore it further.

What?	How?
Why?	When?
Who?	Where?

Then ask the big question: **SO WHAT?**

▶ So... what are the implications? What do these answers tell me about the nature and quality of the source? Can I rely on it?

▶ So... is this source relevant to me and my purpose? How might it be useful to me?

_____

See *Getting critical*, 2nd edn, Ch. 6, in this series.

The research process

Selecting your sources and recording your references systematically starts way back, well before you start planning or writing your assignment.

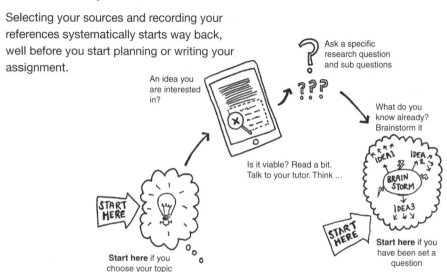

An idea you are interested in?

Ask a specific research question and sub questions

What do you know already? Brainstorm it

Is it viable? Read a bit. Talk to your tutor. Think ...

START HERE

Start here if you choose your topic

IDEA1   IDEA 2

BRAIN STORM

IDEA3

START HERE

Start here if you have been set a question

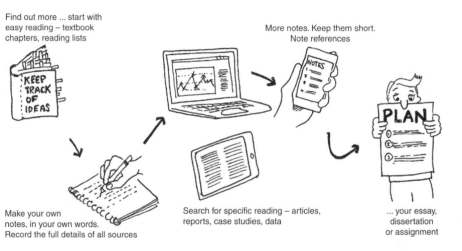

Find out more ... start with easy reading – textbook chapters, reading lists

More notes. Keep them short. Note references

KEEP TRACK OF IDEAS

NOTES

PLAN

Make your own notes, in your own words. Record the full details of all sources

Search for specific reading – articles, reports, case studies, data

... your essay, dissertation or assignment

Referencing tools

A large number of websites and software packages now offer students 'referencing management'. Typically this means that they help students to store, format and make use of references in their texts.

For storage, these websites usually offer both

▶ **manual** recording of sources – where you record each detail yourself on a template, and
▶ **automatic** – where the software saves the details through scanning a code or access to the database.

EndNote

EndNote is a well-established referencing software used in university libraries. When you access sources through library databases, you can export references and store them directly in your own account or 'library'. As you write your assignments, you can cite directly from this library. Endnote online, a free online software, has many of the same functions.

Example from EndNote

The software allows you to cite while writing

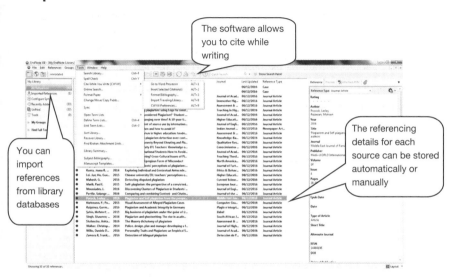

You can import references from library databases

The referencing details for each source can be stored automatically or manually

Software to help you format references can be useful and can save you time, but you still need to check that the formatting is accurate and is in the style your course requires.

Other online referencing tools

Some 'referencing management' tools become more than just managing the references you found. They link to other aspects of research and writing, for example: correcting language and grammar; connecting you to related sources (suggesting that they can cut out any need for further research on your part); or managing social networks.

Be very careful here! Don't cross the line between using a tool to help you with your work as a researcher, and a tool that offers to do the work for you. (See Part 3: Understanding plagiarism.)

Transforming sources into ideas

When you approach your research systematically, recording your references and making notes as you go, you will find that the materials you read gradually shape and transform your thinking. The ideas taking shape in your head have roots back into the material you have read.

Readers want to see both the roots of your ideas, and the value you have added in thinking about them.

In Chapter 4 you can see this in action in an extract that shows a student's research and thinking.

This chapter shows an extract from the literature review of an undergraduate dissertation. Alex, the writer, uses references in a way that shows exactly where he got his information from. He leaves clear footprints:

▶ **in his work**, at the exact point where he uses each source, pointing you to
▶ the **full reference list** at the end, showing you, the reader, where to find each source yourself.

2.1 Mobility cultures

The advent of mass motorisation across western civilisation had a major impact on cycling as an everyday method of transportation. In the UK cycling levels peaked in 1949 when 24 billion kilometres were travelled by bike, 37% of all traffic (Docherty and Shaw 2008) and similarly high levels were experienced in the Netherlands and Denmark (Pucher and Buehler 2008). By the 1970s, cycling had reduced dramatically across Europe: by about two-thirds in a sample of Dutch, Danish and German cities (van Wee, Annema and Banister 2013) and to 1% of modal share of travelling miles in the UK as the car culture dominated transport policies (Sloman 2006).

In the second half of the twentieth century, however, the pattern of cycling in mainland Europe and the UK diverged markedly. Political pressure in the Netherlands led to a dramatic reversal of transportation policy and the re-establishment of the bicycle culture as part of the Dutch national identity (Carstensen and Ebert 2012).

In contrast, no such change in attitudes to cycling has taken place in the UK with its low levels of cycling and poor cycling provision. Horton observes that cycling 'barely registers as a plausible way of moving around' (2011 p48) and overall cycling continues to decline (DfT 2014). Although the number of people cycling to work increased between 2001 and 2011, the proportion remained unchanged at 2.8% of all journeys to work (Office of National Statistics 2011). Aldred and Jungnickel (2014) found that cyclists feel intimidated and 'marginalised' (p80) as road users and argue that policy-makers need to consider local and national cultures and attitudes in planning sustainable transport.

Many thanks to Alex Neisig-Moller (Planning student) for his kind permission to adapt this extract from his dissertation.

Here are the references to sources Alex used in this extract, Harvard style, in alphabetical order by author.

References

Aldred R and Jungnickel K (2014). Why culture matters for transport policy: the case of cycling in the UK. *Journal of Transport Geography.* 34 (Jan) pp78–87. doi: 10.1016/j.jtrangeo.2013.11.004.

Carstensen TA and Ebert A (2012). Cycling cultures in northern Europe. In Parkin J (ed). *Cycling and sustainability.* Bingley: Emerald, pp23–58.

Department for Transport (2014). *Local area walking and cycling statistics England 2012/13*. Available at www.gov.uk/government/uploads/system/uploads/attachment_data/file/306778/walking-and-cycling-statistics-release.pdf (Accessed 29 April 2014).

Docherty I and Shaw J (2008). *Traffic jam: ten years of 'sustainable' transport in the UK*. Bristol: Policy.

Horton D (2011). Don't ride, won't ride. *CTC*. April/May, pp48–51. Available at www.ctc.org.uk/file/member/201105048.pdf (Accessed 12 January 2014).

Office of National Statistics (2011). 2011 Census Analysis: *Cycling to work*. Available at http://webarchive.nationalarchives.gov.uk/20160105160709/http://www.ons.gov.uk/ons/rel/census/2011-census-analysis/cycling-to-work/2011-census-analysis---cycling-to-work.html (Accessed 20 March 2014).

Pucher J and Buehler R (2008). Making cycling irresistible: lessons from the Netherlands, Denmark and Germany. *Transport Reviews*. 28 (4) pp495–528. doi: 10.1080/01441640701806612.

Sloman L (2006). *Car sick: solutions for our car-addicted culture*. Totnes: Green.

Van Wee B, Banister D and Annema JA (2013). *The transport system and transport policy: an introduction*. Cheltenham, Edward Elgar.

The test! Tracking Alex's research footprints

Remember why the reader needs a reference (p4)?

1 Can I, the reader, find the source?
2 What kind of source is it?
3 How does the writer (Alex) use it?

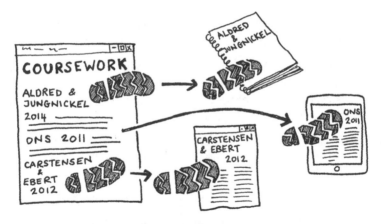

Here is the follow-up to some of Alex's references.

Source 1: Aldred and Jungnickel

Finding it: The Web of Science database via the university library led to the full article. Pre-publication versions or abstracts can be found on Google, Google Scholar, other internet sites, the authors' university, but they may have made changes following feedback from the peer review process. For the definitive version, use an academic database.

Since this article has a doi, is in more than one database, exists in hard copy and is not going to move around, the traditional 'Available at [URL] (Accessed date)' is not necessary.

What kind of source? A highly reliable academic, peer reviewed journal article. Every article in a 'peer reviewed' journal has been read and checked by specialists in the specific research area before publication.

Well used? Yes, very. Alex can rely on this article as evidence for his argument. The authors carried out first-hand ('primary') research themselves and used this to support their argument about cycling culture and infrastructure.

Source 2: Carstensen and Ebert

Finding it: This chapter is in a book edited by Parkin. A search in the library catalogue ('Parkin cycling') listed both the printed book and the eBook (available to view online or download). As they are identical, the writer did not need to specify which version he used.

What kind of source? It's a big (expensive!) textbook, with three major parts, each with several chapters by different authors. Each chapter has its own (useful) references.

Well used? Yes – an excellent start to research with a wide range of specialists and perspectives.

Source 3: Horton

Finding it: 'Page not found'. But the reference had enough details to locate the article quite quickly. The organisation now trades as 'Cycling UK' (spotted at the bottom of the page!). Things do move around and change on the internet.

What kind of source? Cycling UK's online magazine.

Well used? Yes – spot on quote to give a flavour of perspectives from a relevant interest group.

Source 4: Office of National Statistics (ONS)

Finding it: The title was enough to find it immediately via a Google search.

What kind of source? Authoritative government statistics based on the latest census in the UK.

Well used? Yes, very. A primary source for statistics of this sort.

A reference shows your research footprints

- **Printed materials** exist in time and space. The reference gives the information to be able to find it on the library shelf if you are lucky enough to have a library that stocks it – but you don't need to set foot in a library to access most of these materials.
- **Books,** especially popular textbooks, often have their eBook version to read online or download. You can login from anywhere.
- **Academic databases** are the new library shelf – the location is fixed and they don't move around like other online sources. When an article has a doi, you can find that article by typing the doi into a database or search engine.

- The **internet** is vast, mobile and open to everyone. Two points to think about:
  - *Could I or my reader find it again?* Things move around – so include enough details to find it wherever it has moved to.
  - *Is it any good?* Ask questions about anything you find – use the six strategic questions (p5) as a checklist.

Enjoy becoming a researcher!

WRITING AND REFERENCING

Referencing is part of writing for a researcher or student: it's not something you add later. It is through your reading and research that you gain knowledge and understanding, and it is in your writing that you show your thinking. Remember, referencing shows your research footprints (see p26).

Part 2 outlines some of the ways to include your research and reading in your writing – with careful referencing.

Why use the research of other authors?

You may want to:

- use an author as an **authority** to support what you are saying
- introduce someone else's **perspective** that you want to discuss
- provide **evidence** of a trend or development that you are discussing
- show differences between **experts' views** and **interpretations**
- show the difference between an **author's views** and **your own.**

And when do you need to reference?

You need to reference when you:

- use facts, figures or specific details you pick from somewhere to support a point you're making – you **report**
- use a framework or model another author has devised – you **acknowledge**
- use the exact words of your source – you **quote**
- restate in your own words a specific point, finding an argument an author has made – you **paraphrase**

▶ sum up in a phrase or a few sentences a whole article or
chapter, a key finding/conclusion, or a section – you
summarise.

Common knowledge

You don't need to reference if you:
▶ believe that what you are writing is widely
known and accepted as 'fact' or **common
knowledge** in your subject
▶ can honestly say, 'I didn't have to research
anything to know that!'
But
▶ If finding it out did take effort, show the reader
the research you did by referencing it.

Try this!

If you write something down which you can imagine someone else asking
questions about, like 'Really?', 'Who says?', 'Why's that?', 'That's a lot!',
'How do you know that?', then you must have found it out from somewhere,
and you should show your reader where it comes from – in a reference.

Report

When you report on specific information you have found and which you now need to use – like a fact, event, figure, map or date – you bring it into your text, and give the
 - in-text reference, or 'citation'
 - full reference in the references section.

In your work	Reference list
In the UK cycling levels peaked in 1949 when 24 billion kilometres were travelled by bike, 37% of all traffic (Docherty and Shaw 2008) …	Docherty I and Shaw J (2008). *Traffic jam: ten years of 'sustainable' transport in the UK*. Bristol: Policy. It is helpful but not essential to include the page for specific numbers.
… 38% of consumers think that fair trade food is too expensive to buy regularly (Mintel 2015).	Mintel (2015). The ethical food consumer UK. June. Available at file:///C:/Users/Kate/Downloads/The%20Ethical%20Food%20Consumer%20-%20UK%20-%20June%202015%20-%20Executive%20Summary.pdf (Accessed 20 January 2017).

Acknowledge

When you locate a source, it takes a little time to work
out how you will use it. First you have to understand
it, then you engage with it as you think about it. The
Open University (2013) described this progression
as the 'stairway to critical thinking'.

In *Getting critical*, in this series, the idea of a
'stairway' gains an image.

This image is my idea (KW) – but the inspiration
for it came from the Open University. It helped

JUSTIFY
APPLY
EVALUATE
SYNTHESISE
COMPARE
ANALYSE
DESCRIBE   UNDERSTAND
PROCESS

me to organise my ideas for that Pocket book, so it is important to acknowledge the
source. It is also **polite** to **acknowledge** a debt to whoever came up with the model,
template or framework you use – especially if you develop or change it.

Quote

'To copy out or repeat (a passage, statement etc.) from a book, document, speech etc.
with some indication that one is giving the words of another'.

(The Shorter Oxford English Dictionary 2002)

Only use a quote when it is especially important for your reader to see and appreciate the precise wording of the original. You may decide to do this:

1 to provide the reader with the original when you are discussing the text in detail, as in poetry, literary or historical criticism, regulations, reports or policy documents

2 because the writer (or speaker) is eminent/surprising/authoritative

3 because the words themselves are vivid/surprising/a catchphrase and you'd lose the impact if you tried to explain or paraphrase it.

Use quotations sparingly.

George Orwell's advice to writers is as relevant today as it was in the England of the 1940s: 'Never use a long word where a short word will do.' (Orwell 1946 p169). In the 21st century, students …	You can use a quote for any of the situations above. This quote illustrates all three: 1 We (the readers) have the words in front of us 2 The writer is eminent 3 The words are sharp and unique.

Quoted extracts – other people's words – can illustrate a point you make. They are not an alternative to explaining a point in your own words. Using quotes in this way can

▶ give the impression that you don't understand the point well enough to explain it

▶ lock you into describing, and stop you from showing critical thinking in your comments.

Short quotations (less than two lines)

To use short quotes well:

▶ run the quotation into your text so that it reads smoothly

▶ use quotation marks, single or double, as long as you are consistent

▶ give the page number of the original in your in-text reference, so your reader can find it easily

▶ give the full reference in your references section.

In your work	Reference list
Ofsted (2015) states that early years education has an 'unprecedented' political profile and that it has 'never been stronger' (p6). However, the question of who delivers it ...	Ofsted (2015). *Early years annual report*. Available at www.gov.uk/government/uploads/system/uploads/attachment_data/file/445730/Early_years_report_2015.pdf (Accessed 7 December 2016).

Quotation marks are used so your reader can distinguish at a glance between your words and the words of the other writer (or speaker). Your quote must use the exact wording, punctuation and spelling of the original.

See also *Getting critical*, 2nd edn, p76 in this series for 'quote hopping'.

Long quotations (two lines or more)

Typically a long quotation is used for an extract from a key text (for example, a policy document) you want to discuss. To use long quotes well:

 ▸ indent the passage – so no need for quotation marks (don't use them)
 ▸ give the in-text link (citation) to the reference list at the end of the quotation (author-date or numeric), and the page number(s) of the original
 ▸ use […] to show some words have been left out of the quotation
 ▸ give the full reference in the references section.

Avoid going above five or six lines of original text – readers find long extracts too distracting when they are trying to follow your ideas.

The government's strategy to combat childhood obesity stresses the importance of physical activity:

> There is strong evidence that regular physical activity is associated with numerous health benefits for children. The UK Chief Medical Officers recommend that all children and young people should engage in moderate to vigorous intensity physical activity for at least 60 minutes every day. […] At least 30 minutes should be delivered in school every day […] with the

remaining 30 minutes supported by parents and carers outside of school time. (HM Government 2016 p7).

However, if activity in school accounts for only half the amount of recommended time …

Reference

HM Government (2016). *Childhood obesity: a plan for action.* (August). Available at www.gov.uk/government/publications/childhood-obesity-a-plan-for-action. (Accessed 4 February 2017).

Quote + comment

The key thing about deciding to use a quote is:

If it's worth a quote, it's worth a comment!

Don't just drop a quote and run off to your next point. Tell your reader why you think those words are special: what the quote might mean, how it is interpreted, what is interesting/surprising/new/influential about the quoted comment. This doesn't have to be a big deal – see the boxed examples above.

Too much quoting

Generally students quote too much, and comment too little. Do you?

Try this:

- Ask yourself: *Are these **words** (or this extract) somehow special?* If it isn't, then report it, paraphrase it, summarise it – plus comment on it!
- Read a couple of pages from journal articles on your reading list. Count the quotes. Not many? This is telling you something.

As a general rule, if you find yourself quoting more than a couple of words more than once or twice per page or if you find yourself taking a couple of lines from any one source more than once or twice, then you are probably overdoing the quotes. Try and find another way to include the point or discussion. Of course, this does not apply if it's a piece of writing where quoting is half the point, such as an essay about poetry, or discussing a policy document.

Paraphrase

'To express the meaning of (a word, phrase etc.) in other words'.

(The Shorter Oxford English Dictionary 2002)

Paraphrase is about expressing the **meaning** of short extracts – the definition suggests a single word or a short phrase, but it can be longer than this. To express meaning in your own words you first have to understand it, and then find the words to express it.

Paraphrase is hard work. Keep it for short extracts, when the idea is useful to your argument or what you want to say, but the words are not special. Where the words are special, quote (briefly) + comment.

When you paraphrase:

- pick out the key point from the original you want to pay close attention to
- use your own words to restate what the author is saying
- aim to end up with a shorter version than the original
- put the in-text reference as close as you can to your paraphrase, and give the page number(s) of the original
- list the full details in the references
- tell your reader what you want them to see in it – don't just drop it there in the text and run off to your next point!

Example

Jay has read an original source (Eriksen) from his reading list and wants to discuss it in his essay.

Jay wrote ...
Eriksen (2002) comments that the term 'race' is of 'dubious descriptive value' (p4), first, because so many people in the world are of mixed race, and second, because the variation within a single 'racial' group (Eriksen's punctuation) is greater than the variation between different groups.

Reference

Eriksen TH (2002). *Ethnicity and nationalism* (2nd edn). London: Pluto.

The reader sees ...

A close paraphrase of a short section of a paragraph. Key words are quoted: they are 'special' – they sum up the author's view.

Jay explains the two reasons from a longer paragraph in his own words. The reasons are important to understand, but the words of the original are not. By picking the points he shows his understanding – and shortens it.

Problems with paraphrase

Problems often arise when students try to capture summaries by other authors and re-express them in their own words. A textbook or article may summarise the findings or arguments of other studies so that the reader gets an overview of debates or research in that field. The problem for you, the reader, is that you haven't read these other studies, so you don't actually know what they do say – apart from what the text in front of you says they say.

Here paraphrasing is tricky. Without really knowing what the original source said, it is difficult to express it in a different way to how the textbook author put it. This can lead to superficial changes that are, or come close to being, plagiarism.

So try and avoid paraphrasing sources you have not read yourself. Summarise, report on specific findings, and quote + comment on special words. And always show where the ideas came from – with a reference.

See p103 for how to reference a source you find summarised in what you are reading.

See Part 3 for more on plagiarism.

Summarise

'To state briefly or succinctly'.

(The Shorter Oxford English Dictionary 2002)

Summary is key. It is the most efficient way of capturing your research in your writing. Use it if you want to capture, for example:

▶ key outcomes of a study
▶ an argument
▶ the approach taken to X.

First, do your reading. Read a page or two. Look up and think: 'What, in a nutshell, does this tell me that I can use in what I am saying?'

Then write it down, in your own words. Keep it short.

Key steps in making a summary

▶ Pick out the **key points** from the original.
▶ Make your **own notes**, in your own words. When you also include phrases from the original, put them in **quotes in your notes** so you can distinguish between the original (which you will need to reference) and your own comments. Add what you think is important about the point or quote to remind yourself when you come back to it.
▶ **Record full details** of each source.

Then, when you write:

▶ use your own words (of course! The original will be far too long!)
▶ put the in-text reference as close as you can to the summary (before or after)
▶ list the full details in the references
▶ if you are capturing meaning that arises from several pages of reading, you don't need to give page numbers. If you are summarising a specific point from a single page, then give the page number of where exactly you got it from.

Summarising key findings: professionals at work

Below is an extract from a journal article that shows how experienced researchers summarise – in very few words – key findings from other articles to provide evidence for the argument they are making.

Each paragraph in Mills et al.'s article develops one point. String these together, and a series of well-supported and evidenced points quickly becomes an argument.

Summarising shorter sections

You don't have to summarise whole articles in just a few words, of course! You can summarise any material you want to use, with any level of detail you choose. But the process is the same. Ask yourself: what is it they are saying, in short? Is it useful to me? Then bring the point into your work, re-express it in your own words, show where it came from, and comment on it.

The authors wrote ...	The reader sees ...
In sub-Saharan Africa, nurses commonly bear the brunt of health-care delivery, but their numbers have declined substantially in recent years because of migration. In Malawi, for example, there has been a 12% reduction in available nurses due to migration (Ross, Polsky and Sochalski 2005). In 2000, roughly 500 nurses left Ghana, double the number of nursing graduates for that same year (Awases et al. 2004). The recent upsurge in migration has affected the ability of nurse training programmes to continue because of poor staffing levels (Dovlo 2007). Death caused by infectious and chronic diseases (Tawfik and Kinoti 2003) is also a major contributor to nurse attrition in the region.	*In this first sentence (the 'topic sentence') the writers make a clear statement of their point. Then they support their point with evidence from four studies:*
	a key point from a study about Malawi
	a key point from a study about Ghana
	a key point from study about training programmes
	a key point from a study about the impact of disease
	which links back directly to the authors' point in the topic sentence about declining
	numbers of nurses in sub-Saharan Africa.
	It's a well-written paragraph!

Source: Mills EJ, Schabas WA, Volmink J, Walker R, Ford N, Katabira E, Anema A, Joffres M, Cahn P and Montaner J (2008). Should active recruitment of health workers from sub-Saharan Africa be viewed as a crime? *The Lancet*. 371, Feb 23 pp685–88 Doi: 10.1016/S0140-6736(08)60308-6.

Using sources in your writing 51

Using research: Regina at work

Regina is writing an essay on the recruitment and retention of healthcare professionals in the NHS. She is interested in the argument of Mills and colleagues: that recruitment of health workers from poor African countries should be viewed as a crime. A crime? This is strong stuff! Before she draws on their work she has some questions to ask: What evidence do they build their arguments on? Are there other views about this recruitment?

In her discussion of the problem Regina wants to give her reader a more detailed account of Mills et al.'s argument and the wider debate.

The reader sees …

Regina wrote …	
Securing enough health workers to staff UK hospitals has led to recruitment drives in other countries. The practice of actively recruiting from poor African countries, however, has its critics. Mills et al. (2008) argue that current levels of migration from sub-Saharan Africa to developed countries will have 'dire' (p687)	*Topic sentence: Regina outlines the problem of understaffing and recruitment for the NHS in the UK.* *She links this …* *… to Mills et al's argument in a brief summary of their key message.* *She picks out the key point – the 'dire' consequences (strong word, quoted).*

consequences for health in Africa. Based on known patterns of migration in 2004, they project worsening ratios of physicians, nurses and pharmacists 2006–2012 in a population with rising healthcare needs caused by the increase in numbers of people with HIV. In this context Mills et al. describe the loss of skilled personnel through active recruitment by affluent Western countries as 'a violation of the human rights of people in Africa' (p687), and point to various declarations to underline the moral and possibly legal case for ethical recruitment …

More recently, Hidalgo (2013) has argued that recruitment of health workers from low-income countries is 'morally permissible' (p609) …

She summarises a table and a chart to pick out the key messages about loss of skilled health workers and adds in a point from the article about HIV.

She mentions Mills et al. again by name to remind us that we are still reading a summary of their research, and quotes a powerful key phrase.

She doesn't list all the policies and legal agreements, but focuses on the way Mills et al. use them to make their argument and links this back to HER point in her topic sentence – about NHS recruitment.

New paragraph, new point. Regina introduces another aspect of the debate in her topic sentence.

Regina's references for this extract

Hidalgo JS (2013). The active recruitment of health workers: a defence. *Journal of Medical Ethics*. 39, pp603–9. doi:10.1136/medethics-2012-100927.

Mills EJ, Schabas WA, Volmink J, Walker R, Ford N, Katabira E, Anema A, Joffres M, Cahn P and Montaner J (2008). Should active recruitment of health workers from sub-Saharan Africa be viewed as a crime? *The Lancet*. 371, Feb 23 pp685–8.

Summary is *the* most useful skill in writing about your research. Combined with short quotes it gives a powerful flavour of the research you are reading, and offers a ready way for you to draw material into your argument.

6 Write with confidence

Regina (p52) and Alex (Chapter 4) are both capable student writers. As readers we are interested in what they have to say. This chapter takes a close look at the strategies, structures and language a writer can use – and inspire confidence in their readers.

Putting references in your text

As soon as your reader starts thinking these things, then as a writer you have a problem. You need to get in quicker and show your reader whose ideas you are writing about.

Whose writing is this?

Is this my student or Blockelbicker?

Where is this coming from?

Try this:

- Show your source before your reader starts to wonder whose work they're reading!
- If your account of what an author said continues for more than a couple of sentences, repeat the author's name to remind your reader that they are reading your version of what someone else says. (Look back at the extract from Regina's essay – half way down she puts in a reminder that she is still talking about Mills et al.'s research.)

Two styles for writing (in Harvard)

Style 1: Focus on the *ideas*

In this writing style, you want to focus on the ideas and research findings that provide evidence for your argument. The author(s) name does not naturally appear in your writing so you add the author(s) and year in brackets to show the reader where ideas or evidence comes from. The brackets hardly interrupt the flow, and academic readers are well used to this.

Below is the extract from Mills et al. again, this time with the key points shown in bold, and the in-text references just there in brackets.

In sub-Saharan Africa, **nurses** commonly bear the brunt of health-care delivery, but their **numbers have declined** substantially in recent years because of migration. In Malawi, for example, there has been a 12% reduction in available nurses due to **migration** (Ross, Polsky and Sochalski 2005). In 2000, roughly **500 nurses left Ghana**, double the number of nursing graduates for that same year (Awases et al. 2004). The recent upsurge in migration has affected the ability of **nurse training programmes** to continue because of poor staffing levels (Dovlo 2007). **Death caused by infectious and chronic diseases** is also a major contributor to nurse attrition in the region (Tawfik and Kinoti 2003).

Source: Mills et al. (2008 p685), with bold added for emphasis.

Style 2: Focus on the *source*

In this writing style, you want the reader to be more aware of the authors/researchers (as well as their findings or ideas). Below is the same extract rewritten to show the change in emphasis. Here you naturally mention the author(s) names as part of the text. You add the year in brackets to pinpoint the sources listed in the reference list. You need to use words to introduce the research – also shown in bold.

In sub-Saharan Africa, nurses commonly bear the brunt of health-care delivery, but their numbers have declined substantially in recent years because of migration. **Ross, Polsky and Sochalski (2005) found** that in Malawi, there has been a 12% reduction in available nurses due to migration. **Awases et al. (2004) calculated** that in 2000, roughly 500 nurses left Ghana, double the number of nursing graduates for that same year. **Dovlo (2007) describes the impact of** the recent upsurge in migration on the ability of nurse training programmes to continue and **attributes** poor staffing levels **to** this migration. Death caused by infectious and chronic diseases has been **identified by Tawfik and Kinoti (2003)** as a major contributor to nurse attrition in the region.

Source: Mills et al. (2008 p685), minor amendments, and bold added.

Your choice

When you write, use whichever style seems to fit most naturally in your sentences, and feel free to move between them in the same piece of writing.

The word count factor

- Style 2 (focus on the source) is about 10% longer than Style 1.
- Style 1 (focus on the ideas) is about 10% longer than the numeric style (see Vancouver, Part 5).

These figures are inflated because we have used the extracts to illustrate points, but it is worth noticing that numerical referencing styles are generally more economical with words.

Introducing sources

The language used to introduce the various studies and their authors in the Style 2 extract is active. The writers (Mills et al.) are telling the reader what they think the authors are **doing** in the articles they report on.

> Ross, Polsky and Sochalski (2005) **found that** … Awases et al (2004) **calculated that** … Dovlo (2007) **describes the impact of** … and **attributes** … to … **identified by** Tawfik and Kinoti (2003)

The choice of verb to introduce a study is a key strategy for indicating what you want to say about the source. It is satisfying to the reader (especially if they are your tutor!) to see from your choice of verb that YOU can see what authors are DOING in writing up their research.

Six magic verbs

Smith (2013)	points out argues maintains claims concludes suggests	that	preventative medicine is far more cost effective, and therefore better adapted to the developing world

Source: University of Manchester (2016). This is a tiny extract from this excellent resource for language to use in academic writing.

Try it!

Try using these words to introduce research into your work. You'll see how powerful they are in changing and shaping meaning. Use them to say what you mean. Use them carefully!

Using 'state': don't!

Nicholson (2015) states that empowerment gives the employee the power and authority to do things at work.

> Well does it?
> Or not?
> What evidence do you have either way?

All this tells your reader is that you have read Nicholson (probably) but you have absolutely nothing to say about it! It can lead to noncommittal 'descriptive' writing.

Only use when

you present a statement by an author, often an organisation, which you then go on to discuss and examine:

Ofsted states that early years education has an 'unprecedented' political profile and that it has 'never been stronger' (p6). **However, the question of who delivers it ...**

How sure are you?

Researchers are careful about their use of language when they write up their research.

Tentative	Definite
Emerging research	Established findings

When 'new knowledge' begins to emerge, researchers are cautious and tentative about their conclusions. They only make statements for which they feel the evidence is sound:

> *There is the possibility that …*
> *He also suggests that …*
> *Studies indicate that …*

As knowledge in a field becomes more established, the debate moves on:

> *Dissenbak (2012) maintains …*
> *Two recent studies (Clogg and Klee 2014; Ballard 2013)*
> *challenge …*

And as 'knowledge' becomes confirmed by further studies, more categorical statements can be made:

> *Konrad (2015) found/demonstrated/showed that …*

The key point here for you is: DON'T OVERSTATE! Only be as definite in your language as the evidence allows you to be – and choose your words accordingly.

And if you want to show differences?

If you want to show differences between the views and interpretations of experts in the field, or between an author's views and your own, your **choice of verb** can show how close or distant you are to the views or findings of an author.

Distant	Close
Cohn (2015)	
claims that …	
discussed the idea …	
asserts …	
considers …	
contends …	
observed that …	
points out …	
reported …	
has shown …	
demonstrated …	
confirms that …	

Have something to say: use your topic sentences!

Using research in your writing isn't just about the techniques for referring to your sources – crucial though this is. It is about having something to say about what you've learnt; showing your line of reasoning, your position on something.

Look at how Alex used topic sentences to structure his argument in his dissertation (p27).

2.1 Mobility cultures

The advent of mass motorisation across western civilisation had a major impact on cycling as an everyday method of transportation. In the UK cycling levels peaked in 1949 … ◄

Alex's major point, his core argument, in the first topic sentence. It drives the whole section.

He starts to show the evidence that underpins this point.

In the second half of the twentieth century however, the pattern of cycling in mainland Europe and the UK diverged markedly… ◄

The second major point in the topic sentence. Evidence follows.

In contrast, no such change in attitudes to cycling has taken place in the UK with its low levels of cycling and poor cycling provision… ◄

Third major point in the topic sentence (and evidence follows). Each step makes the focus of his argument – and dissertation – clearer.

Regina too makes HER points arising from her research in the topic sentence of each paragraph (pp52–3).

The take-away point?

The topic sentence in each paragraph is where YOU make the statements you want to make. The evidence follows. This is the route to becoming a confident writer – with something to say.

UNDERSTANDING PLAGIARISM

Part 3 is designed to help you understand plagiarism so that you can avoid it, and also understand what you are doing and how to use sources effectively.

Of course, some plagiarism is deliberate. Students who pay someone to do the work or blatantly cut and paste or copy others' work have not learnt anything. When they hand in work, they are claiming: 'Here's my assignment'. Quite plainly it isn't, and quite plainly this is cheating. This guide is not about that sort of plagiarism.

This guide is for students who do their own work and want to take credit for it, but are worried that they don't understand plagiarism and might slip into it by accident. Part 3 explains what plagiarism is and how to make the right decisions to avoid it.

What is plagiarism?

There is no quick answer to this as there are many aspects to plagiarism. At university, plagiarism involves a set of steps:

> **A student**
> ▶ takes something such as the work, words or ideas
> ▶ from someone else* such as an author of a journal article, a website, an organisation, another student, a family member
> ▶ and then puts it into their own work – essay, presentation or dissertation
> ▶ as if it were their own work, or without making the source clear, or making clear the distinction between their own work and others' work.

* See also explanation of self-plagiarism at the end of Chapter 7.

Good academic practice

Understanding good academic practice is just as important as understanding plagiarism: it's the other part of the picture. Just focusing on what you must not do does not necessarily guide you to what you need to do. Good academic practice is about how you carry out your work from start to finish, step by step.

- Really understanding the task before you start
- Doing your research: from lecture notes, then reading lists and independent research
- Planning, constructing and preparing your assignment yourself
- Taking information from sources from your notes (and some quotes, if needed)
- Recording all references for in-text citations and the reference list
- Citing sources in your text in the right place so your links are clear
- Writing the assignment in your own words.

What is my own work?

Many courses require students to sign a sheet saying the work is their own. You must have ticked dozens of boxes on websites to say you've read the terms and conditions (really?). But what are you signing up to when you sign: 'This is my work'?

WORK not words!

We are talking about WORK here, not just about words. Parts 1 and 2 describe some of the work involved in writing good assignments: identifying sources, taking notes, linking your sources with your points and arguments ... for starters. Then there's the work of turning your ideas into words and the work of putting the whole thing together as a cogent piece of text. All that most definitely adds up to WORK!

This is what you are being assessed on. This is what you take credit for – and this is a major route by which you learn.

Learning: the point of it all

Tutors design courses, assignments and 'learning experiences' which they think will promote learning. They also have to make sure that the rules are followed and that anyone who gets credit for achieving something does so by the rules and plays fair.

The 'rules of the university game' might be explained like this.

> We don't give credit for students doing the assignment. We give credit if students learn something by doing the work we set.

What's the difference?

Look at the following two tables to see the difference.

A student hands in an assignment that shows ...	What's going on?
'I took care of seven people with emphysema.'	That's doing something OK, but that's all it is.
'I took care of seven patients with emphysema and here is a care plan about the best ways to take care of patients with emphysema which I found in my textbook.'	That's not learning, that's doing something and copying. And they don't connect. Is the care any better for having read the textbook? There's no evidence of it.
'Two months ago, I could not have made a care plan for a patient with emphysema. Now I have taken care of seven and read some books and talked with people who know about it and, now, here's my care plan.'	That's learning, and the plan shows the work that went into the learning. It is based on the evidence of other people's work in the field, informing your own ideas and approach.

In this last example you are **applying** what you learnt. You can only do this when you fully understand, have thought about it and relate it to your own circumstance. Applying is near the top of the 'stairway to critical thinking'.

See p39 and *Getting critical,* 2nd edn, p14 in this series.

Your own work

For work to be your own, you need to do some thinking and express yourself, according to your views, knowledge, understanding and research. Think about whether the following students are doing **their own work**.

They say it so much better than I can

A student describes what she did for her assignment	What's going on?
I found some really good information in a table from two websites, and I copied the statistics and the analysis to make my argument.	That does not show your learning or understanding or any interpretation, and may also be plagiarism if the sources are not cited correctly.
I based my assignment around quotations from sources which I cited. Some of the ideas were really hard to understand so I left them as quotes.	This is not plagiarism but it is overreliance on sources so your own voice is hidden. Basing an assignment around quotes makes it look as if you have not understood. It is important to understand the ideas that you are using and to write in your own words.
I got some information from sources and compared them and showed the reasons why I agreed with some of them.	Good practice – getting information from a range of sources, comparing and then using them to show your thinking.

Note on self-plagiarism

You need to be clear when you can and cannot use your own work a second time. Self-plagiarism is taking your own work that you previously submitted for credit and reusing it (all or parts) to submit for credit another time.

This is not about drafts of work you produce on the way to a final piece, or early work that feeds into later submissions (both completely acceptable and expected), but where you reuse a previously submitted assignment for a different course or module when you should be submitting new work.

You can only get credit for a piece of work once!

When you first start working on an assignment, you may be thinking: It has to be 'my own work'. Does that mean no one can help?

No. You can and should ask others for help and advice when you need it. But what kind of help is acceptable?

Here's a simple test about asking for advice: Are you asking for advice or help so **you** can do the work? Or do it better? If the answer is 'yes', then that's fine.

Or is the 'help' really about getting someone else to do the work **for you**? This is not OK.

DO ask tutors or university study advisers for advice.

Don't hesitate! Just ask – it's what they are there for.

Getting advice early on is always a good idea – it kick-starts your understanding of what the assignment is asking you to do, and can help you with planning your work.

What other sorts of help can you use?

1 Help with looking for sources

YES	NO
▶ When someone shows you how to locate sources or use databases. ▶ If using others' research to trigger your own: for example, tracking down the references from another source.	▶ If it means someone else doing the searching and choosing for you.

2 Help with writing citations and references

YES	NO
▶ If you are checking against available guides and trying to format correctly.	▶ If you are relying on referencing tools to do your research and find sources for you. If you use these tools in this way, you won't be actively thinking about your assignment (see Chapter 3).

3 Consulting classmates about your work

YES

▶ Discussion is a great way to shape your own ideas. If you are *not* talking to people about your subject, you are really missing out!

▶ And especially yes when discussion sends you back to do more thinking and research.

NO

▶ If you just swallow other people's ideas and copy them as if they were yours ('without attribution').

▶ Sharing files of work with classmates – this is an invitation to copy and will land both the sender and receiver in trouble.

Getting help with writing

A huge range of websites and tools are available to help with academic writing, so you need to make good decisions about the use of these tools. Think about the following:

Paraphrasing tools

A number of websites offer paraphrasing, usually free. They provide a box for you to submit a text and then they produce a new text from your submission. This can mean the tools are rewriting a source text or writing your text for you.

YES	NO
▸ Check individual words you can't find synonyms for, although you might be able to do this more effectively with dictionaries/thesaurus tools, or from your own vocabulary.	▸ Don't upload your texts to tools – this takes away your control of the text.

Example

We uploaded the phrase below about Bhutan (see pp90–1 for full extract and reference) to some free online paraphrasing sites. See what happened!

Source text		Comments on paraphrasing by tools
Bhutan was the first country in the world to pursue happiness as a state policy.		
Paraphrasing tool 1	Bhutan was the <u>principal nation</u> on the <u>planet</u> to <u>seek after bliss</u> as a state <u>approach</u>.	This tool paraphrases word by word with apparent synonyms, but some have different meanings: *principal* for *first*, *world* for *planet*, *happiness* for *bliss*, *policy* for *approach*. *Seek after bliss* sounds very unnatural.
Paraphrasing tool 2	Bhutan was the <u>primary nation</u> on the planet to <u>seek after joy</u> as a state <u>arrangement</u>.	This tool paraphrases in a similar way to no.1, again with some differences in meaning: *primary* for *first*, *joy* for *happiness*, *arrangement* for *policy*. It also sounds unnatural.
Paraphrasing tool 3	Bhutan <u>might have been those To begin with nation on the universe will seek after satisfaction Likewise a state approach</u>.	This tool paraphrases in unconnected phrasal blocks, which make the new text unintelligible. Some blocks also begin with capital letters which make it very confusing to the reader.

Plagiarism checking tools

Of the many plagiarism checking tools available now, Turnitin (Feedback Studio) is the one used by most universities (see Chapter 10), but students often want to find a way to check plagiarism online themselves:

YES	NO
▶ Use Turnitin and get advice on use of sources from your tutor (see Chapter 8 on Turnitin). WriteCheck (the online Turnitin service for students) could also be used for a fee.	▶ Don't upload your work to online checking tools! The check may be inaccurate and they may even make use of your assignment for themselves!

Translation tools

You can translate source material from one language to another fairly easily using Google Translate or other online translation services.

YES	NO
▶ If you check with your tutor who agrees you may use some sources in translation (properly cited and translated).	▶ If you use texts in other languages and translate them without citing, or without making clear what is your own work and that of other authors.

Example

To test translation tools, we uploaded the phrase above onto Google Translate and translated it into German, then back into English.

Source text		Comments
If you use texts in other languages and translate them without citing, or without making clear what is your own work and that of other authors.		
Google Translate into German	Wenn Sie Texte in anderen Sprachen verwenden und sie ohne Anführungszeichen übersetzen oder ohne klar zu machen, was Ihre eigene Arbeit und die anderer Autoren ist.	The translation follows the original, but changes 'citing' into 'quotation marks'.
Google Translate from German back into English	If you use texts in other languages and translate them without quotes, or without clarifying what your own work and the other authors are.	Notice that now in the English version, 'without citing' has been changed into 'without quotes', which means something completely different! The last phrase 'what your own work and the other authors are' is vague and ungrammatical, and does not show the meaning of the original.

Language tools

Language tools help you to correct your grammar, spelling or style.

YES	NO
▶ Check for basic grammar.	▶ If you use language tools to completely edit and rewrite your work.

Example

We uploaded the student text below, which contains a number of grammatical errors, to two online language tools.

Student text		Comments on language correction by tools
In conclusion research show that, the rapid growth of low cost airlines in the UK also change UK traditional rules about air travel. Companies have to balance many goals and most important thing is companies' value creation. To reach their optimal position, Bargainair must keep flow cost. This study show that lowcost airlines, their difficulties with overcome example		
Language tool 1	In conclusion research <u>show</u> that, the rapid growth of low cost airlines in the UK also <u>change</u> UK traditional rules about air travel. Companies have to balance many goals and ∧ most important thing is <u>companies' value creation</u>. To reach their optimal position, Bargainair must keep flow cost. This study <u>show</u> that lowcost airlines, <u>their</u> <u>difficulties with overcome example</u>	This tool underlined errors and added comments beside, eg 'it appears that the verb should be in the past tense'. The tool did not underline errors in vocabulary, eg 'flow cost'.
Language tool 2	In conclusion, this research has shown that the rapid growth of low cost airlines in the UK seems to have changed UK rules about air travel. In balancing many goals, companies develop a primary objective of value creation. To reach their optimal position, Bargainair must keep the flow cost. This study has shown that difficulties may occur with challenging opportunities.	This tool corrected and rephrased the original text, in a similar way to the paraphrasing tools. Some corrections changed the meaning of the original text. Some errors remain, eg 'flow cost'.

So, language tools might help you gain awareness of grammatical errors. That's good! Then you can correct them. But if you use them simply to make your work better, without any effort from you, then you are not doing your own work. Be an active learner and keep improving yourself!

> But it says it's plagiarism free!

Help from essay writing tools

There are a huge number of essay writing sites which offer to write your essay for you. They also suggest they can 'help' you write.

NO! Only NO for this one. This is not your work! Universities take a very strong line against these sites which compromise the authenticity of student work. Don't use these websites for anything. They may have free essays or samples available or offer you 'tutorials' to help with your work, but any use of these websites is likely to lead to problems. Keep away!

Think about where you draw the line between acceptable practices and plagiarism.

Do the quiz below, thinking about how you work on your assignments. Each example puts you in the situation of a student working on an assignment and needing to make decisions about avoiding plagiarism. Imagine it is you and decide what is acceptable and what could be plagiarism.

Quiz 1: Acceptable practice?

	Question: Is this acceptable? Why/why not?	**Answer** Yes/No
1	You have to write a research paper. You read an article which cites other articles that you do not actually read. The author of the article you do read has summarised them. You list both the article you have read and the ones you haven't in your references and use them all in your text.	
2	You are not confident about writing assignments in your own words. You know that Turnitin can find website matches, so you think it will be safe to copy some sections from an old textbook on your subject. You think the language will be better than yours, so you might get a higher mark.	
3	You go to an art gallery and make sketches of six pictures, then take elements from each one as inspiration for your own picture. Then you hand in your own.	
4	You are struggling with an assignment. As your friend took the same module last year and she is a very good student, you ask her for help. She sends you her assignment and you use it for the structure, references and main sections of your assignment.	

5	You decide to write about the same topic that you are very interested in, for two different modules taught by different teachers. You don't tell the teachers. You use most of the same sources and some of the same paragraphs for each, but write each assignment following the task.	
6	You are running out of time to submit your assignment and very worried about fulfilling the 2,000 word count requirement. You decide to copy in some sentences from websites to fulfil the word count.	
7	You ask someone to proofread and improve the language in your essay before you hand it in. You hope this will improve your grade.	
8	You do not have time to read sources. You write your own ideas and add citations next to them, without reading the sources. You do not think the tutor will notice.	
9	You find an essay written in another language that you understand and you decide to translate it for your own essay. You use your own words for the translation and include the citations the author used, but you do not cite the author of the essay.	
10	You are getting very stressed about marks. You start looking at websites which offer you help with writing your essay. They say that what they do is 'plagiarism-free' so you can't get into trouble.	

Now check your answers with ours shown upside down on the next page.

Answers to Quiz 1: Is it acceptable?

7	Tricky. To what extent is it still 'your own work'? Grammar checking is generally considered acceptable for someone else to help you with, but if the checker went beyond that and improved your language, it could be plagiarism. The only person who should be trying to improve your grades is you!
8	NO. This is unacceptable and your tutor is very likely to notice. This is a form of falsification.
9	NO. Translating into your own words does not make the ideas yours. Not citing the original article also makes this plagiarism. It seems as if you are trying to hide the source!
10	NO. This is a dangerous area. Don't believe what essay writing sites tell you. They may suggest that they can help you make an assignment (or write it completely for you) which is 'plagiarism-free', but this usually means they claim it will circumvent Turnitin. Getting help in this way is a very serious form of plagiarism and could mean you are expelled from the university.

1	NO. Don't use the reading and work of other authors as if it were your own. If you want to cite a source, you need to read it yourself.
2	NO. Not getting a match on Turnitin does not mean your assignment is 'plagiarism-free'. Copying from other sources, new or old, is plagiarism, and your tutor will be able to tell. Also, it does not sound as if the source will be useful!
3	YES. This is absolutely fine – it is what art students should be doing in their sketchbooks.
4	NO. If you use your friend's work in this way, then your assignment will not be your own. Discussing some ideas or getting some recommendations for sources would be OK, but making direct use of sections of another's text is definitely not acceptable. Your friend is also likely to be in trouble for directly sharing her work with you.
5	NO. This is self-plagiarism or duplication as you are trying to get two marks for one piece of work. Unless you have two assignments which form part of a whole, as set out in task instructions, you cannot reuse your assignments in this way (see p74).
6	NO. Of course, it is important to follow word count, but it is more important not to plagiarise! Copying to fill in words for an assignment is not acceptable.

Quiz 2: Where do you draw the line?

Quiz 2 is about good practice when you describe research in your work. Read the following extract and assess how it is used.

Bhutan was the first country in the world to pursue happiness as a state policy. The Bhutanese concept of happiness is deeper than the common meaning of happiness in industrialized countries. The philosophy of gross national happiness has several dimensions: it is holistic, recognizing people's spiritual, material, physical or social needs; it emphasizes balanced progress; it views happiness as a collective phenomenon; it is both ecologically sustainable, pursuing well-being for both current and future generations, and equitable, achieving a fair and reasonable distribution of well-being among people. Since the early 1970s, Bhutan has promoted population well-being over material development. Happiness, health and well-being are closely related. Good health is often considered the single most important determinant of well-being; conversely, adverse health changes have lasting and negative effects on well-being.

In industrialized countries, happiness is often linked with material consumption. A basic level of material wealth is necessary, but citizens of richer and more technologically advanced countries are not necessarily the happiest. Along with economic growth, there is a need to measure well-being and ecological sustainability to reflect the overall progress of nations and of humankind. Given increasing evidence that the current trajectory of human development is not sustainable, there is an urgent need for more inclusive measures of progress than traditional economic indicators such as gross domestic product.

Source: Sithey, G., Thow, A.-M. and Li, M. (2015). Gross national happiness and health: lessons from Bhutan. *Bulletin of the World Health Organization*, 93(8), p514.

Four student writers used the text above in an essay on the relationship between happiness and wealth. Decide for each whether the use is the right side or the wrong side of the line between good academic writing and leaning too heavily on someone else's work.

1	The Bhutanese concept of happiness is deeper than the common meaning of happiness in industrialized countries. Since the early 1970s, Bhutan has promoted population well-being over material development. In industrialized countries, happiness is often linked with material consumption. A basic level of material wealth is necessary, but citizens of richer and more technologically advanced countries are not necessarily the happiest.

2	Sithey, Thow and Li (2015) describe the policy towards gross national happiness in Bhutan. They make the point that in industrialized countries, happiness is often linked with material consumption. Given increasing evidence that the current trajectory of human development is not sustainable, there is an urgent need for more inclusive measures of progress than traditional economic indicators such as gross domestic product.
3	There appears to be a big contrast between Bhutan and industrial countries. Bhutan has a policy of holistic happiness but in industrial countries "happiness is often linked with material consumption. A basic level of material wealth is necessary, but citizens of richer and more technologically advanced countries are not necessarily the happiest" (Sithey, Thow and Li 2015: 514). The government of Bhutan pursue happiness as a state policy.
4	Sithey, Thow and Li (2015) define the key aspects of Bhutan's concept of happiness as prioritising wellbeing but also covering holistic needs, having a collective and fair approach, developing in a balanced way and including ecological sustainability. These aspects are in contrast to happiness in industrialised countries where it tends to be connected to material wealth, and perhaps as a consequence, where people are less happy.

These are our comments on the examples above.

1	This is just copy and paste. Although the writer has chosen sentences from different parts of the text, they are copied word for word, so this is clearly plagiarism and does not show any learning.
2	This writer starts by citing the article to start creating their own message, which is good, but then falls back on too much copying. The reader will definitely notice complex words like 'trajectory' and will start to wonder whose work this is.
3	This writer makes a good effort to use the text by starting with a clear topic sentence which summarises the main point. The quote, however, does not seem necessary and is too long. Words need to be special for a quote (see P40) and the writer should always comment on it. Some words in the last sentence are copied. Despite its faults, this writing is acceptable.
4	This is an effective summary of the key points, reformulated in a different order, showing the contrast between Bhutan and other countries, and showing an understanding of the message of the source text. It's a good piece of writing.

Turnitin (Feedback Studio), the electronic text matching tool, is now used by most universities worldwide. Understanding plagiarism at university includes understanding some things about Turnitin.

What can you see on Turnitin?

▶ Coloured matches to uses of the same words in the same order as other texts.
▶ Calculations of percentages representing how much of the submitted work can be matched to other texts (overall amount and breakdown of individual matches).

The extract below shows the matching of a source text, ranked 5, calculated as 1% of the work submitted by the student.

Example 1: SMEs

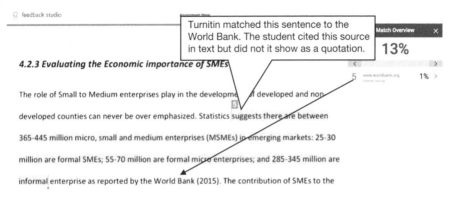

Do the matches mean plagiarism?

No, the matches do not necessarily mean plagiarism. It means that the submission has similarities to other texts. If these texts are properly cited, with appropriate quotation formatting where necessary, and references given, then it is not plagiarism. Too much textual similarity may indicate a problem of overreliance on other sources, but this is not plagiarism if the above conditions are met.

Example 1 above clearly shows where the information is from (World Bank 2015), but should have used the formatting for quotations '…'.

Sometimes there are matches to standard academic phrases (like 'the aim of this study is to evaluate …'), which anyone might use when introducing a study. These matches are not plagiarism – they are good practice!

The following extract shows some use of standard phrases in an abstract.

Example 2: Social media marketing

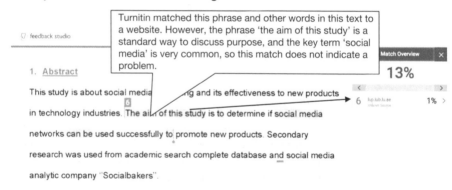

Turnitin matched this phrase and other words in this text to a website. However, the phrase 'the aim of this study' is a standard way to discuss purpose, and the key term 'social media' is very common, so this match does not indicate a problem.

feedback studio

Match Overview ×

13%

1. Abstract

This study is about social media ……ng and its effectiveness to new products

in technology industries. The aim of this study is to determine if social media

networks can be used successfully to promote new products. Secondary

research was used from academic search complete database and social media

analytic company "Socialbakers".

6 lup.lub.lu.se 1% >

Other matches may include the task title or instructions, the institution address, the list of references; none of these are plagiarism either.

Matches on Turnitin do indicate plagiarism if larger sections of text (ie, two or more sentences) have been copied without citation or '...' (quotation marks). Inadequate paraphrasing can also show up on Turnitin and could be considered plagiarism where the student's text is too similar to the source text. Even where there isn't a continuous match, Turnitin shows up strings of words with gaps.

Example 3: Green roofs

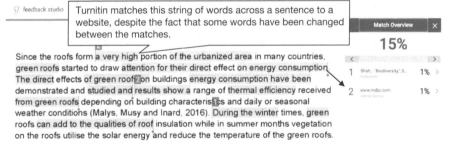

In this example, the string shows up text with four gaps 'a very high ... of the urbanized area ... green roofs ... attention for their direct ... on energy consumption', showing the student's reliance on the structure of the source text.

What should you do about the matches?

Discuss with a tutor or adviser and make sure you fully understand about how you are using sources, what mistakes you may be making, what you need to revise and what you can leave as it is. Do NOT get the idea that you need to 'make the colour go away'. Matches can indicate both good practice and plagiarism, so you need to make sure you distinguish between matches to change and matches to leave.

Apart from Turnitin

Your reader has other means of telling if it is your work:

▶ **style changes**: the language used by student writers, published writers and random web sources is usually quite different
▶ **mix of referencing systems**: some numeric, some author-date, some with no references at all, or unusual references
▶ **oddities in expertise**: when a complicated problem, say, or very advanced methodology is dropped into a piece of work without explanation.

What to remember about plagiarism

Use **'I am doing my own work'** as your guiding principle to decide what is OK and what is not OK when you are writing assignments.

▶ It is basically OK when you are actively engaged in researching, preparing, structuring, citing, paraphrasing, summarising and writing your assignment.
▶ It is not OK when you are not actively engaged because you are borrowing too much from other authors or you are getting others, or other tools, to do your work for you.

REFERENCING: THE PRACTICALITIES

Part 4 starts with answers to frequently asked questions about referencing (Chapter 11). Chapter 12 gives examples of how to reference essential sources: books, journal articles and websites, and Chapter 13 provides additional examples of frequently used sources.

All examples show how to cite the source in your text and list it in your reference list.

References or bibliography? What's the difference?

In Harvard and many other referencing styles (APA, Chicago author/date, Vancouver), the **Reference list** or **'References'** is a list of all the sources you have referred to in your writing. This is what most tutors require.

A **bibliography** is a list of everything you have read on a subject, including background reading, whether you refer to it or not. You may occasionally be asked for a bibliography (of your reading to date); for example when your tutor wants to see where you have got to in your research for a dissertation proposal.

If you are asked for a bibliography for a finished piece of work, divide it into two sections:

1 *References:* for sources you cite in your text
2 *Other sources consulted:* for materials you have read but chose not to use.

Tutors sometimes use the term 'Bibliography' to mean 'Reading list' or 'Suggested reading'.

Some other referencing styles (including MHRA, Chicago NB and Oscola) refer to the list of 'references' at the end of a piece of work as a 'bibliography'. This often lists all the sources you cite in footnotes and endnotes, pulling it all together in one list.

How do I reference a source I found in a book/article but I haven't actually read it myself?

The answer is simple. You only list something in your references if **you have actually read that source**. You list the text where *you* found it in your references list, and refer to the actual source in your work. This is called **secondary referencing**.

In your work	Reference list
Herzberg's two-factor theory of motivation at work (Herzberg, Mausner and Synderman 1959 cited in Mullins 2016 pp232–3) drew attention to job design …	Mullins LJ (2016). *Management and organisational behaviour* (11th edn). New York: Pearson.

In this example, you haven't read Herzberg et al., but you have read the chapter in Mullins, your textbook, which summarises and discusses Herzberg et al.'s theory. You cite Herzberg et al. in your text (with page numbers) and point your reader to where you found it (Mullins) – so they can find it too.

A primary source is information collected and written up by the organisation or person who carried out the work at first hand: data collection, a case study, observations, theory, analysis.

Secondary sources are written by someone who has read the primary source and described it in some way. A textbook is a secondary source that includes a lot of references to primary sources. An article may review other research (so here it's a secondary source) before going on to report on the authors' own primary research.

Tertiary sources are collections or summaries of other sources: encyclopedias, directories, dictionaries, Wikipedia. They are useful to orientate you on a topic but not close enough to the original primary research to be useful as evidence in your writing.

Use primary sources wherever you can, and be careful about relying too heavily on secondary sources. A textbook or article that summarises a lot of work in the field is a good place to start for an overview. However, if you don't go and find the actual sources, your understanding of the study, data or whatever is limited to the short summary you find in the textbook. You may then have to paraphrase someone else's summary (see pp45–7). If you do this a lot, it will be clear to your reader that you have only read the one textbook as this is the only one you can list in your references.

However, when the original is hard to find (eg, it is old, or has restricted circulation) and you want to use it because it is special in some way, do so as in the boxed example above.

When do I put in page numbers?

The test for adding page numbers is simple: if what you are referring to came from a particular page, then give the page number. It makes it easier for the reader to pinpoint, and shows how organised you are as a researcher.

- Any quote will come from a particular page, so give the page number(s).
- If a figure or illustration you refer to comes from a specific page, then give the page number(s).

If you are referring to a general idea, or summarising a whole section or chunk, then don't give the page number(s) – your reader will need to read more to understand the material.

Why do authors put in a string of references?

You are most likely to see a string of references at the beginning of an article, in the introduction. The authors may want to refer briefly to **well-established research findings**, and then to move on swiftly to the issues that concern them.

> Cycling conditions in most countries – including the UK and the USA – are anything but safe, convenient and attractive (Pucher et al. 1999; McClintock 2002; Pucher and Dijkstra 2003; Tolley 2013).

Or they may want to give an overview of research on **different aspects** of the topic before they move on to their focus.

> ... it is well accepted that oral language skills underpin successful reading comprehension (Clarke et al. 2010, Mutter and Lindgren 2007, Stenseth et al. 2010). Research on reading in ASD has focussed on investigating a small subgroup ... (for reviews and recent findings, see Grigorenko et al. 2003, Keenan 2001, Semel et al. 2009).

Note that these extracts order their citations differently. The first lists them by date of publication (oldest first), the second by alphabetical order of author.

The same author has several publications in the same year

When you want to refer to several articles or documents by the same author all published in the same year, you need to be able to show your reader which is which. This most often happens with a:

▶ weekly journal or newspaper when a journalist writes regularly on the same or similar topics
▶ government or official body that issues statements, guidelines, reports or policies on a regular basis.

In your work	Reference list
You show which is which by adding a letter to the year:	Organisation for Economic Co-operation and Development (2016a) (+ full details).
The aim of the Forum (OECD 2016b) was to quantify the links between the environment and economic growth.	OECD (2016b). *Global Forum on Environment.* Available at www.oecd.org/greengrowth/greeneco/ (Accessed 19 January 2017).
	OECD (2016c) (+ full details).

When do I use 'et al.'?

'Et al.' is a shortening of the Latin 'et alia' which means 'and others'. It is used in referencing when there are multiple authors, more than is sensible to write out in your text, or (a matter of judgement) in your reference list.

In your work	Reference list
Use et al. with four or more authors:	List all authors:
Mills et al. (2008) argue that current levels of migration from sub-Saharan Africa …	Mills EJ, Schabas WA, Volmink J, Walker R, Ford N, Katabira E, Anema A, Joffres M, Cahn P and Montaner J (2008). Should active recruitment of health workers from sub-Saharan Africa be viewed as a crime? *The Lancet.* 371, Feb 23 pp685–8. doi: 10.1016/S0140-6736(08)60308-6.
(See Regina's essay, p52)	

Harvard has no single authoritative handbook, so advice varies. Our advice credits all authors with their contribution, from the first named, the lead author (often an eminent professor), to the last, a researcher, perhaps a PhD student.

It especially matters in relation to the **citation rate** and **analysis** which is an indicator of its contribution to the field.

> **The citation rate** counts the number of times an article is cited by other works. At 137 the Mills et al. article has evidently been influential in the field.

Here's another reason to list all authors in the full reference: this team of researchers includes experts from across continents – universities in Canada, South Africa, Uganda and Argentina and from Médecins Sans Frontières, the medical charity. Their purpose is to mount and evidence a persuasive argument: the profile and status of the authors strengthens this.

> **Who** wrote it?
> How are they qualified?
> What is their expertise?
> How valid is their evidence?
> **So how** might I use this source?

Thinking about the expertise of authors is, of course, an important element in your critical evaluation of your reading. Good referencing is the first step to becoming a reflective and 'critical' researcher and writer.

12 Essential sources and examples

This chapter gives examples of references from the most frequently used sources: books, journal articles and internet sources (Harvard style).

How to reference a book

3 *Title of book*   4 *Edition*

THIRD EDITION

HEALTH STUDIES

AN INTRODUCTION

1 *Author/s (or editor/s)*

EDITED BY
JENNIE NAIDOO & JANE WILLS

© Selection and Editorial Matter: Jennie Naidoo and Jane Wills 2015
Individual chapters © contributors 2015

All rights reserved. No reproduction, copy or transmission of this
publication may be made without written permission.

No portion of this publication may be reproduced, copied or transmitted
save with written permission or in accordance with the provisions of the
Copyright, Designs and Patents Act 1988, or under the terms of any licence
permitting limited copying issued by the Copyright Licensing Agency,
Saffron House, 6–10 Kirby Street, London EC1N 8TS.

Any person who does any unauthorized act in relation to this publication
may be liable to criminal prosecution and civil claims for damages.

The authors have asserted their right 2 × *Year of*
work in accordance with the Copyright, Des *publication (of*

First edition 2001
Second edition 2008   *3rd edition)*
Third edition 2015

First published 2001 by
PALGRAVE

Palgrave in the UK is an imprint of Macmillan Publishers Limited, registered
in England, company number 785998, of 4 Crinan Street, London N1 9XW.

Palgrave Macmillan in the US is a division of St Martin's Press LLC,
175 Fifth Avenue, New York, NY 10010.

Palgrave is a global imprint of the above compani 5 *City of*
throughout the world.

Palgrave® and Macmillan® are registered trademarks in th *publication*
6 *Publisher*   , Europe and other countries.
ISBN: 978–1–137–34867–8

This book is printed on paper suitable for recycling and made from fully
managed and sustained forest sources. Logging, pulping and manufacturing
processes are expected to conform to the environmental regulations of the
country of origin.

A catalogue record for this book is available from the British Library.

A catalog record for this book is available from the Library of Congress.

Typeset by Aardvark Editorial Limited, Metfield, Suffolk.

The six points of a book reference
1 **Author**(s) or **editor**(s) as shown on the title page: family name/surname first, followed by initial(s)
2 **Year** of publication (in brackets). Give the date of the edition you are using
3 **Title** of the book in *italics*
4 **Edition** (if not first)
5 **Place of publication** (city/town/state)
6 **Publisher**

In your work	Reference list
Obesity impacts on many aspects of health and wellbeing (Naidoo and Wills 2015) psychological as well as physical …	Naidoo J and Wills J (eds) (2015). *Health studies: an introduction* (3rd edn). London: Palgrave.

Books can be written by individuals. Organisations can also be the author.

Book references

In your work	Reference list
One author	
The poorest children in sub-Saharan Africa are 4.5 times less likely to have primary schooling than the richest (UNICEF 2014).	United Nations Children's Fund (UNICEF) (2014). *The state of the world's children 2014: every child counts.* UN Distributed Titles: New York.
	This report is also available at www.unicef.org/sowc2014/numbers/documents/english/SOWC2014_In%20Numbers_28%20Jan.pdf (Accessed 20 January 2017).
Two authors	
Wetherly and Otter (2014) argue that as people experience a globalising world as tourists, business too is …	Wetherly P and Otter D (2014). *The business environment: themes and issues in a globalising world* (3rd edn). Oxford: Oxford University Press.

Three authors	
… the argument that education is no longer a guarantee of future earnings (Brown, Launder and Ashton 2012) …	Brown P, Launder H and Ashton D (2012). *The global auction: the broken promises of education, jobs and incomes.* Oxford: Oxford University Press.

Four or more authors	
Slow-twitch fibres in muscle perform a different function to fast-twitch fibres (Sadava et al. 2013 p1007).	Sadava DE, Hillis DM, Heller HC and Berenbaum M (2013). *Life: the science of biology* (10th edn). Sinauer: Sunderland, MA.

A chapter in an edited book

In your work you refer to the author(s) of the chapter you are using. Your reader looks for this name in your references, and sees the book it is in.

In your work	Reference list
The case study used by Ogden (2015 p147) suggests that beliefs about food and the individual's experience of eating are powerful factors in …	Ogden J (2015). Health psychology. In Naidoo J and Wills J (eds). *Health studies: an introduction* (3rd edn). London: Palgrave. pp113–50.

eBooks

▸ When an eBook looks like a printed book, and has all the details of a printed book, reference it like a printed book (see p32).

▸ If the eBook does not have the format or details of a printed book, then take your reader to it.

In your work	Reference list
This behaviour is similar to … (Meldrum and Frith 2016).	Meldrum E and Frith ML (2016). *Animal cognition: evolution, behaviour and cognition* (3rd edn). CourseSmart. Available at: www.coursesmart.com/animal-cognition-2nd-edition/ clive-d-l-wynne-monique-a-r-udell/dp/9781137367297 (Accessed 20 February 2017).

Page for your notes and references

How to reference a journal article

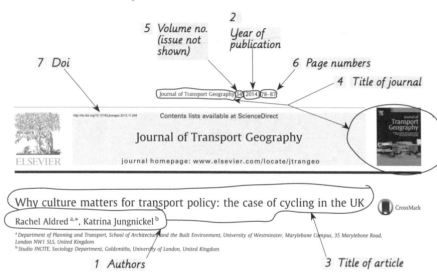

5 Volume no. (issue not shown)

2 Year of publication

7 Doi

6 Page numbers

4 Title of journal

Journal of Transport Geography 34 (2014) 78–87

http://dx.doi.org/10.1016/j.jtrangeo.2013.11.004

Contents lists available at ScienceDirect

Journal of Transport Geography

journal homepage: www.elsevier.com/locate/jtrangeo

ELSEVIER

Why culture matters for transport policy: the case of cycling in the UK

CrossMark

Rachel Aldred [a,*], Katrina Jungnickel [b]

[a] Department of Planning and Transport, School of Architecture and the Built Environment, University of Westminster, Marylebone Campus, 35 Marylebone Road, London NW1 5LS, United Kingdom
[b] Studio INCITE, Sociology Department, Goldsmiths, University of London, United Kingdom

1 Authors

3 Title of article

The seven points of a journal reference

1 **Author**(s) in the order shown: family name/surname first, followed by initial(s)
2 **Year** of publication (in brackets)
3 **Full title of article**
4 **Title of journal** in *italics*
5 **Details**: volume/issue/month (where given)
6 **Pages** of the article
7 **DOI (Digital Object Identifier)**

When there is no doi use:
Available at [URL] (Accessed + date)

Your reader can find the article with details 1–6 above – this is enough.

In your work	Reference list
Aldred and Jungnickel (2014) found that cyclists feel intimidated and 'marginalised' (p80) as road users …	Aldred R and Jungnickel K (2014). Why culture matters for transport policy: the case for cycling in the UK. *Journal of Transport Policy*. 34 (Jan) pp78–87. Doi.10.1016/j.jtrangeo.2013.11.004

For referencing purposes, there is no distinction between online journal articles (that only exist online) and journal articles that exist in print but you find online.

The question for you is whether the article has a doi or not:

▶ Where an article has a doi, you can find it by typing the doi into a database or search engine. The details 'Available at [URL] (Accessed + date)' are not relevant or needed.

▶ Where there is no doi, show the route you took: Available at [URL] (Accessed + date).

In your work	Reference list
One author	
The future of nurse training programmes in these poor countries is precarious ... (Dovlo 2007).	Dovlo D (2007). Migration of nurses from sub-Saharan Africa: a review of issues and challenges. *Health Services Research*. 42 pp1373–88. Doi: 10.1111/j.1475-6773.2007.00712.x.

Two authors	
The debate about the best approach to increasing cycling continues (Aldred and Golbuff 2012) with integrationists pointing to …	Aldred R and Golbuff L (2012). *Cycling Policy in the UK: A Historical and Thematic Overview*, University of East London. Available at http://rachelaldred. org/wp-content/uploads/2012/10/ cycling-review1.pdf. (Accessed 15 January 2017).
Three authors	
Dillig, Jung and Karl (2015) argue that renewables did not actually push up the price of electricity in Germany but filled important gaps […] and brought the price down.	Dillig M, Jung M and Karl J (2015). The impact of renewables on electricity prices in Germany – an estimation based on historic spot prices in the years 2011–13. *Renewable and sustainable energy reviews*. 57 pp7–15.
Four or more authors	
Budget hotel cooperatives in Malaysia made a significant contribution to the economy (Kamal et al. 2017).	Kamal R, Sheriff MH, Abadin Z and Faik HS (2017). Malaysian budget hotel cooperatives. *International Hotel Management*. 11(3) pp23–32. Doi:10.3932/ibm.2016.5182.5189.

How to reference an internet source

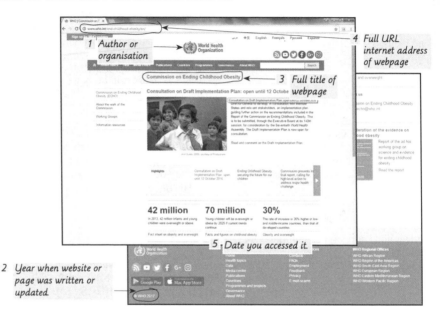

1 Author or organisation

4 Full URL internet address of webpage

3 Full title of webpage

5 Date you accessed it.

2 Year when website or page was written or updated.

Five points of an internet reference

1 **Author**(s) of the website (organisation or person)
2 **Year** the website or page was written or updated
3 **Full title** of the webpage or site (in *italics*)
4 **Available at** www ... (URL)
5 **(Accessed ...)** + date on which you accessed the specific page

In your work	Reference list
The WHO (2017) identifies a number of specific actions to prevent childhood obesity, involving ...	World Health Organization (WHO) (2017). *Commission on ending childhood obesity*. Available at www.who.int/end-childhood-obesity/en/ (Accessed 2 February 2017).

If any of the above details really are missing, then include those you do have. Do some strategic thinking though: what is this source floating around cyberspace with no visible author or organisation? Who wrote it? How did they do the research/produce the policy? So ...

> How reliable is the information? Can I use it?

You will by now have identified a broad pattern to the information you need to record in a reference for any source you use. A reference is the answer to the **strategic questions** you ask yourself about any source you encounter:

Who wrote it?

When was it published?

What is the source? The title? What kind of source is it?

    1 Author(s)   *2 Year*   *3 Title of article*

Aldred R and Jungnickel K (2014). Why culture matters for transport policy:
the case of cycling in the UK. *Journal of Transport Geography.* 34 (Jan) pp78–87.
doi:10.1016/j.jtrangeo.2013.11.004

  7 Doi   *4 Title of journal*   *5 Volume + Issue*   *6 Pages*

How was it published? What kind of 'host'?

Where did **you** find it? (and where can **I** find it?)

You can adapt this to any source you need to reference. It will include some, probably not all, of these.

▸ **Author** (person/s or organisation)	▸ **What kind of item?** Film/DVD/press release/advertisement/theatre
▸ **Year** of publication	
▸ **Title of item** you are reading or viewing	▸ **Title of 'host'**: book/journal/website/ collection/database
	▸ **Helpful details** to locate the item: in print/online/in a physical location.

For online materials, add

▸ **doi** where there is one (generally for articles)

For all other online materials

▸ **URL + Date you** accessed it.

This chapter includes more models you may be able to use and adapt.

Be confident! Work at it and if you really can't find a model for a particular item, generate it from the outline (and thinking) above. Present all your references in a consistent order and style. The point is to be transparent about what your source is, and helpful to your reader if they want to track it.

Newspapers and magazines

In your work	Reference list
Danish and US scientists are alarmed by the high sea temperatures and record low ice formation (Vidal 2016).	Vidal J (2016). 'Extraordinarily hot' Arctic temperatures alarm scientists. *The Guardian*. Available at www.theguardian.com/ environment/2016/nov/22/extraordinarily-hot-arctic-temperatures-alarm-scientists (Accessed 17 January 2017).

Brochures, posters, leaflets

If you pick up a brochure, poster or leaflet, it may be helpful to say where this was. If you want a copy, look online.

In your work	Reference list
Following a number of high profile deaths of cyclists, the Department for Transport (no date) urged cyclists to 'hang back' …	Department for Transport (no date). *Don't get caught between a lorry and a left turn: hang back.* [Cycle safety stand, Reading city centre] 4 December 2016. or Available at http://think.direct.gov.uk/cycling.html (Accessed 5 December 2016).

Reports and company documentation

In your work	Reference list
The supermarket Morrisons recognise that turning around the business will take time (Morrisons 2016).	Morrisons plc (2016). *Annual report and financial statements 2015/16.* Available at www.morrisons-corporate.com/annual-report-2016/pdf/Morrisons_AR_2015_Web_Full.pdf (Accessed 4 December 2016).

Statistics

In your work	Reference list
Britain now supplies 17.8% of electricity demand by renewable energy in comparison to 28.2% in Germany (Eurostat 2016).	Eurostat (2016). *Share of energy from renewable sources.* Available at: http://ec.europa.eu/eurostat/web/products-datasets/-/nrg_ind_335a (Accessed 3 March 2017).

Theses and dissertations

In addition to the standard details, it is helpful to add where the thesis or dissertation can be found (eg, a library or collection). If you access the thesis online, add the 'Available at [URL] (Accessed + date)' details.

In your work	Reference list
Transposing cycling infrastructure from one country to another is not the obvious solution it might at first seem (Neisig-Moller 2014). It has to …	Neisig-Moller A (2014). *Build it and they will come: the role of segregated 'Dutch style' bicycle infrastructure in Stevenage new town in getting people cycling.* MSc thesis. Oxford Brookes University. Unpublished MSc dissertation. Oxford Brookes University.

Course materials

Lecturers prefer you not to reference course materials (PowerPoint, course handbooks), because they want you to go off and follow up some of their suggestions on the reading list. If, however, you do use course materials as your source of information, say so – it is misleading not to.

Add Available at [URL] (Accessed + date) if this is expected. If you have to login to your institution's VLE (virtual learning environment) to access these materials, nobody outside your course could access them, so logically there is no point in adding these details.

Tutor notes

In your work	Reference list
In the case study of Café Direct, Grebenik (2016) proposed a framework for …	Grebenik D (2016). Week 5 Ethical business case study. *Module Handbook U61321 Business in context.* Business School, Southern University.

PowerPoint presentation

In your work	Reference list
One definition of learning is the ability to think and reason (Swarbrick 2016). This underpins the other definitions …	Swarbrick N (2016). Child Centred Teaching and Learning [PowerPoint presentation] *Week 10 U70124 Outdoor Learning.* Oxford Brookes University.

Audiovisual material

TV and radio

In your work	Reference list
The ingenuity of animals in surviving in the harshest conditions on earth (Deserts 2016) is powerfully captured in …	Deserts (2016). *Planet Earth 2.* Episode 4. BBC1 Television. 27 November.

Film/video/YouTube

Film: in your work	Reference list
The modern take on the style of old Hollywood musicals gives *La La Land* its … (*La La Land* 2016).	*La La Land* (2016). Directed by Damien Chazelle [Film]. United States: Summit Entertainment.

YouTube: in your work	Reference list
Many people will recognise themselves in Tim Urban's description (2016) of not getting things done …	Urban T (2016). *Inside the mind of a master procrastinator*. Available at www.ted.com/talks/tim_urban_inside_ the_mind_of_a_master_procrastinator (Accessed 20 January 2017).

Photo/image

In your work	Reference list
The young wildlife photographer of the year Gideon Knight (2016) demonstrated that a world class photo can be taken in the local park.	Knight G (2016). *The moon and the crow.* London: Natural History Museum. Available at www.nhm.ac.uk/visit/wpy/gallery/2016/images/15-17-years-old/5138/the-moon-and-the-crow.html (Accessed 5 December 2016).

Personal communications

The primary purpose of referencing personal communications is to record and evidence your research trail in your project, not to enable your reader to track back to the source. It may be more appropriate to include a transcript/edited key points/email printout as an appendix.

In your work	Reference list
Citation	
FitzGerald (2017) offered some additional insights into …	FitzGerald J (2017). Conversation [or email/text/letter/phone/Skype conversation] with/to Brenda Laycock, 13 April.

Link to appendix	Appendix 1: Email correspondence
One branch manager commented on the difficulties of … (see Appendix 1)	Joe FitzGerald: 13 April 2017 or Branch Manager A (if anonymity required)

Social media

Blogs

Blogs (weblogs) and vlogs (video logs) are in effect open online conversations between the blogger and anyone who cares to join in. You cannot use them as 'evidence' of anything other than what they are – personal views and experiences (often very interesting!). Use the name or alias.

In your work	Reference list
Co-living, with private rooms and communal workspaces, is an example of opportunities for young freelances and startups to … (Bearne 2016)	Bearne S (2016). Espressos and networking: co-living has me hooked. *Guardian small business network*, 4 Dec. Available at www.theguardian.com/small-business-network/2016/dec/04/espressos-networking-co-living-has-me-hooked (Accessed 11 December 2016).

Twitter

In your work	Reference list
Reporting from war zones is no longer the preserve of war reporters – the people involved, even children (see Bala Alabed 2016 for example), have their voice …	Alabed B (2016). [Twitter] 6 December. Available at https://twitter.com/AlabedBana?ref_src=twsrc%5Egoogle%7Ctwcamp%5Eserp%7Ctwgr%5Eauthor (Accessed 6 December 2016).

Part 5 outlines four other (non-Harvard) referencing styles:

▶ In-text numerical styles: Vancouver (Chapter 14) and MHRA (Chapter 15)
▶ In-text author styles: APA (Chapter 16) and MLA (Chapter 17).

It works by showing an extract of work using the style with annotations pointing out:

▶ how to make the link in the text (citation)
▶ where footnotes are used, how to detail a source here
▶ how to set out references in the reference list (or bibliography or Works Cited).

Look closely at the annotations – these offer useful specific guidance.

A simple search for any particular style will take you to various university library websites. Check two – but be prepared for variations. Even within guidance to the same style, individual course/module handbooks, institutions, journals and online advice will vary. So:

- get the general idea of how to use a style (from this book)
- find out which style you are asked to use
- use any guidance you are given in your course materials
- find a good set of models
- stick to it for consistency.

For more guidance on the styles above plus Chicago and Oscola (law), see the latest edition of *Cite them right* or the electronic version *Cite them right online* via your university library.

Vancouver: in-text numeric style + References in number order

Vancouver is most commonly used in science, medicine and related subjects. The numeric style focuses the reader's attention on the research. References have logical but minimal punctuation and no unnecessary words to distract from the communication between scientists.

Vancouver numeric referencing style works like this:

- **In your work** use a number in superscript[3] or brackets, round (3) or square [3], at the point where you draw on a source.
- **In your references** give the full details of each source in numerical order, with the first source you use listed as 1, the second as 2 and so on.

Below is an extract (adapted) from the article by Mills et al. (see Chapter 5) using the Vancouver numerical reference style of the original.

In the article

> ... the UK has over 100 times more physicians than Malawi[3] and the consequences show in the mortality rates.[4, 5] ...
>
> In sub-Saharan Africa, [numbers of] nurses have declined substantially in recent years because of migration. [...] In Malawi, for example, there has been a 12% reduction in available nurses due to migration.[14] The recent upsurge in migration has affected the ability of nurse training programmes to continue because of poor staffing levels.[15]
>
> The number of pharmacists in sub-Saharan Africa is very low. Liberia has a pharmacist-to-population ratio of only one to 85,000,[3] 77 times lower than in the USA.[3]

> Adapted with thanks from Mills EJ, Schabas WA, Volmink J, Walker R, Ford N, Katabira E, Anema A, Joffres M, Cahn P and Montaner J. Should active recruitment of health workers from sub-Saharan Africa be viewed as a crime? *Lancet.* 2008; **371**: 685–88. doi: 10.1016/S0140-6736(08)60308-6.

Reference to source 3 in the reference list

References to two sources supporting this point

Reference to another study with points of relevance to the argument summarised in brief

Further references to source 3

All authors listed. You have the option of using 'et al.' after listing six authors (see p108)

Selected references for this extract

3   World Health Organization. Human resources for health 2007. www.who.int.whosis/indicators/2007HumanResourcesFor Health/en/ (Accessed 27 Nov 2007).

4, 5 (Not detailed here)

14   Dovlo D. Migration of nurses from sub-Saharan Africa: a review of issues and challenges. *Health Serv Res*, 2007. **42**:1373–88. doi 10.1111/j.1475-6773.2007.00712.x

3 Organisation as author, referred to three times in the extract
- *Name in full*
- *Title of source (online)*
- *URL*
- *Date accessed*

4, 5 Evidence to support a point

14 Journal article (exists in print)
- *One author*
- *Title of article (standard text)*
- *Title of journal in italics (shortened)*
- *Year of publication*
- *Volume of journal in **bold***
- *Page numbers just as numbers*
- *Doi always welcome*

15 MHRA style
Modern Humanities Research Association

MHRA: in-text numeric style + footnotes in number order + Bibliography

This referencing style is used in some arts and humanities subjects. It allows readers to see immediately the source of information or to get a glimpse of a discussion point on the same page as the text.

The citation in the text makes the link to the footnote with a **number**, usually in **superscript**[1].

Sources are first shown in **footnotes** at the bottom of the page, in the order in which they occur throughout the essay or article, or, less often, as **endnotes** at the end. All sources, and other sources read but not cited, are collected together in a full **bibliography** at the end.

This example has been written to show how this referencing style works. It is not a good piece of writing, and has far too many references!

The popularity of the cinema peaked in the 1940s and 1950s.[1] It remained above 1,000 million between 1940 and 1955.[2] Precise figures about audiences are hard to come by,[3] but it is clear that the majority of cinema-goers were women.[4] Hollywood carried out research that established that women wanted 'good character development' and 'human interest'.[5] The films produced by Hollywood at this time were 'strongly feminised'[6] and appealed to their largely female audiences for their 'glamour'[7] … Some women watched particular films – such as *Calamity Jane* – countless times …[8]

In your footnotes (or endnotes)	Your footnotes explained

In your footnotes (or endnotes)

Your footnotes explained

1 Pat Fisher and Piers Madison, *The Cinema Compendium,* (London: British Film Association, 1999), pp219–20.

A book (first mention), full details:
- *First names before surnames for up to three authors;*
- *'and others' for four or more authors*
- *Title in italics*
- *Other details in brackets (place of publication, publisher, year)*
- *Page number(s) last: p for one page, pp for more than one page*
- *Commas used throughout and full stop at the end*

2 Ibid., p209.

'Ibid' is short for the Latin 'ibidem' meaning 'in the same place'. It refers to the source immediately before (Pat Fisher and Piers Madison)

3 For a useful collection of facts and figures of cinema-going Britain, see Melvyn Wallerstein, 'Going to the pictures: the changing social experience', *The Cinema Journal*, 35 (2001), 103–115.

This is a short discussion of the difficulties of finding reliable information, and refers the reader to a book listed in the bibliography (Wallerstein), but not cited in the text

4 *The Cinema Compendium*, p225.

This is a quick referral back to a source already cited in full

5 Ibid., p220.

This refers to The Cinema Compendium again. See (1) for full details

6 Frank Dubon, *Hollywood Revisited,* (New York: Studio Panorama, 2004), p158.

Another source, full details

7 Ibid., p167.

This refers to the source immediately above – Dubon

8 These films have provoked considerable debate among ...

This is the beginning of a lengthy note summarising the discussion among commentators

In your bibliography at the end, you collect all the sources from your footnotes, and list them in alphabetical order.

Bibliography

Dubon, Frank, *Hollywood Revisited,* (New York: Studio Panorama, 2004)

Fisher, Pat and Piers Madison, *The Cinema Compendium,* (London: British Film Association 1999)

Wallerstein, Melvyn, 'Going to the pictures: the changing social experience', *The Cinema Journal*, 35 (2001), 103–115

Your bibliography explained

Note the 'hanging indent': the first line of each work cited goes to the margin, and the rest is indented.

A book, one author, with full details:
- *Surname first (first name in full or initials)*
- *Title in italics*
- *Other details in brackets (place of publication, publisher, year)*
- *No page numbers*
- *Commas used throughout, no full stop at the end*

A book, two authors
Full details as above except surname first for first author, then first name first for second and third authors

Journal article
This article is not directly referenced in the essay, but was used as background reading. Include it in the bibliography, with full details:
- *Author, surname first*
- *Title of article in single quotation marks*
- *Title of journal in italics*
- *Details in brackets (volume/issue)*
- *Year of publication*
- *Page numbers*
- *Give the doi if it has one (see* p117 *)*
- *For ejournals, give the URL like this:*
<wwwjstor.org/stable/644897> [Accessed 27 March 2017]

16

APA style
American Psychological Association

APA: in-text author/year + References in alphabetical order

This style is used in subjects related to psychology and in some other social science subject areas. It is very similar to Harvard. The extract and comments below illustrate where APA is **different** to Harvard.

In your work

> ... oral language skills underpin successful reading comprehension (Garcia, Martin, Gauson & Misra, 2012; Lopez & Hulme, 2014). The National Institute for Reading (NIR) (2015) set out the evidence for early engagement with picture books. Lopez and Hulme argue that talking about picture books enables children to make the transition to reading .... Garcia et al. underline the importance of ...
> Children who have experience of wordless picture books have learnt to read images (Keenan et al., 2011), a skill they carry into ...

Your in-text references explained

Three to five authors
- List all in your text the first time you refer to them with the last linked by '&'
- Later citations, shorten to first author followed by 'et al.'

One or two authors
- Give the surname (for one), or both surnames (linked with & for two) throughout your work

Organisation as author
- Give name in full the first time you mention it, and by initials for subsequent citations

- Use 'and' (not '&') to link two authors when the names fall naturally in the sentence
- No need to repeat the year of publication when you refer to the same author in the same paragraph

Six or more authors
- Too many to list in the text
- Shorten to first author's surname + 'et al.' throughout

References

Note the 'hanging indent': the first line of each work cited goes to the margin, and the rest is indented

Garcia, P., Martin, S.G., Gauson, M.D. & Misra, K.B. (2012). Talk first: laying the foundations for reading. *Reading research, 35(7)*, pp346–78. DOI: 10.1288/0945167331057081

Keenan, F., Muter, S.R., Linden, K., Schmitt, R., Johnson, J. & Elster, M.A. (2011). Assessing reading comprehension in young children. In A. Goodman (Ed.), *Learning the language* (pp77–95). Boston: Parton.

Lopez, J. & Hulme, P.G. (2014). Making the story: transitions in young readers. *The reading journal, 28(5)*, pp106–30.

National Institute for Reading (NIR) (2015). *Teaching reading: an evidence based assessment of strategies for teaching reading*. Retrieved from www.nir.org.uk/data/teachread/file/pdf

Your reference list explained

Journal article
- *Three to five authors, last linked with '&'*
- *Year of publication (in brackets)*
- *Title of article*
- *Title of journal + volume and issue in italics*
- *Where the doi is given, no other identifier or access details needed*

Chapter in book
- *Six authors, the maximum given in full before using et al.*
- *Year*
- *Chapter title*
- *In*
- *Author or editor of book with initial(s) first. Note (Ed.) or (Eds.)*
- *Title of book in italics*
- *Pages*
- *Place of publication: publisher*

Organisation as author/online report
- *Name of organisation in full and by initials*
- *Title of publication in italics*
- *Retrieved from [URL] No date given*

17

MLA style
Modern Language Association

MLA: in-text author/page + 'Works Cited' in alphabetical order

This style is used in arts and literature subjects where detailed discussion requires precise and repeated referencing, often to specific quoted phrases.

The **citation in the text** is the **author** and **page number**, making the link to the **Works Cited** (not References) listed in alphabetical order by surname at the end.

In your work

> In *Mrs Dalloway*, Virginia Woolf's characters encounter each other … In response to his questions, Clarissa seemed "contracted, petrified" (70) but moments later …
>
> Claire Levenson (43–44) draws attention to the 'real world' of Britain between the wars in which …
>
> … the suggestion that Clarissa's identity as Mrs Dalloway was 'somehow incongruous' (Toller and Geraets 184) has led to discussion as to whether …

Works Cited

Levenson, Claire. "Women between the wars or between the acts?" *The Sussex Review*, vol. 35, no. 4, 2012, pp73–89. JSTOR, www.jstor.org/stable/43607145.

Works Cited explained

Note the 'hanging indent': the first line of each work cited goes to the margin, and the rest is indented.

The source: journal article
- *Author: surname first (first name in full)*
- *Title of article: double inverted commas beginning and end*

Container 1: print details
- *Title of journal in italics*
- *Details (volume/issue/page nos)*

Container 2: where you found it (Database)

Toller, Susan and
Michael Geraets. "A
life in a day." *Virginia
Woolf: reality and
fiction*, edited by
Robert T. Magnani,
Eagle, 2009,
pp169–83.

Woolf, Virginia.
Mrs Dalloway.
Penguin,1992.

The examples above are based on the guidance in the 8th edition of the MLA Handbook (2016). The aim of this book is 'rethinking documentation for the digital age' (back cover). It focuses on the principles and purpose of referencing, rather than rules for setting out a reference for every type of source – those already in use and into the future.

The 2016 MLA style recognises that sources are mobile: editions and locations change constantly as texts are republished, included in collections, placed online and so on. In referencing, one size will not fit all into the future.

The AUTHOR and TITLE OF SOURCE are unique. Beyond this the MLA describes everything as being a 'Container' – the details of where you actually found the source you are using.

The point of this revised system is to give you a **template** to record how YOU found the source, so writers (that's you!) can make their references useful to their readers. Because the template aims to be flexible and comprehensive, you will leave many sections blank.

Here is how it works for the first source listed above.

1 Author. Levenson, Claire.	
2 Title of source. "Women between the wars or between the acts?"	
CONTAINER 1 These are likely to be print details	CONTAINER 2 These are often the digital details
3 Title of container, *The Sussex Review*,	3 Title of container, JSTOR,
4 Other contributors,	4 Other contributors,
5 Version,	5 Version,
6 Number, vol. 35, no. 4,	6 Number,
7 Publisher,	7 Publisher,
8 Publication date, 2012,	8 Publication date,
9 Location. pp73–89.	9 Location. www.jstor.org/stable/43607145.

Rather than stressing about the 'correct' way to list sources you can't find a model for, the aim of the new MLA system is to encourage you to:

- ▶ **THINK** and evaluate each source
- ▶ **SELECT** and gather the information about a source from the answers to these questions
- ▶ **ORGANISE** how you create your documentation from the text itself.

And **WHY** do you do this? The answer, as the MLA puts it, is to enable 'readers to participate fully in the conversations between writers and their sources' (2016 xii).

This, in essence, is what referencing is about.

Enjoy the conversation!

References

Godfrey J (2014). *Reading and making notes* (2nd edn). Basingstoke: Palgrave Macmillan.

Godfrey J (2016). *Writing for university* (2nd edn). London: Palgrave.

Godwin J (2014). *Planning your essay* (2nd edn). Basingstoke: Palgrave Macmillan.

Modern Language Association of America (2016). *The MLA Handbook* (8th edn). New York: MLA.

Open University (2013). Critical thinking. © The Open University.

Pears R and Shields G (2016). *Cite them right* (10th edn). London: Palgrave.

University of Manchester (2016). Referring to sources. *Academic Phrasebank*. Available at www.phrasebank.manchester.ac.uk/referring-to-sources/. (Accessed 15 January 2017).

Williams K (2014). *Getting critical* (2nd edn). Basingstoke: Palgrave Macmillan.

Useful sources

Academic Phrasebank www.phrasebank.manchester.ac.uk

Cite them right online (the online version of Pears R and Shields G (2016). *Cite them right*. London: Palgrave) is available via many university libraries

Davis M (2011). Plagiarism quiz for Bailey, S. *Academic writing: a handbook for international students* (3rd edn) [Online]. Available at http://cw.routledge.com/textbooks/bailey/questions.asp?unit=1

Godfrey J (2016). *Writing for university* (2nd edn). London: Palgrave.

Indiana University How to recognize plagiarism; tutorials and tests

www.indiana.edu/~academy/firstPrinciples/choice.html

Leeds University Academic integrity & plagiarism advice

https://library.leeds.ac.uk/skills-academic-integrity

Monash University Plagiarism advice

www.monash.edu.au/lls/llonline/writing/general/plagiarism/5.xml

WriteCheck Writing Center resources for students

http://en.writecheck.com/resources

Index